Table of Contents

Appendix begins after page 40.

Introduction

This handbook is intended to assist claims examiners in the identification and development of survivor claims that involve potential common-law marriages (these are informal relationships that can sometimes be legally recognized as valid marriages) filed under the Energy Employees Occupational Illness Compensation Program Act of 2000 (EEOICPA). EEOICPA provides that when a covered employee is deceased at the time benefits are to be paid, payment is to be made to the employee's eligible survivors. Thus, in order for a survivor to be entitled to EEOICPA benefits, he/she must provide evidence proving their relationship to the employee.

Claimants can assert entitlement to EEOICPA benefits as the employee's surviving spouse by virtue of a common-law marriage. The issue of the existence of a common-law marriage most often arises when a claimant asserts eligibility for survivor benefits due to his/her status as the employee's surviving spouse, but where no licensed marriage ceremony took place. The second most common occurrence is where the claimant and the employee were legally married less than one year prior to the employee's death, but the claimant asserts that they entered into a common-law marriage before the legal marriage that satisfied EEOICPA's one-year marriage requirement. Another variant of the common-law marriage situation exists where the claimant asserts that he/she and the deceased employee were once legally married, then dissolved their marriage, and then reunited to establish a common-law marriage prior to the employee's death.

The common thread running through each of these types of claims is that the eligibility of the claimant turns, in part, on whether a common-law marriage was established between the deceased employee and some other person and whether that marriage was created at least one year prior to the covered employee's death. In all of these cases, claims examiners must adequately develop the evidence of all required elements of a common-law marriage before the eligibility determination can be made. This handbook provides information and general guidance to assist claims examiners in their development of common-law marriage claims. The information in this handbook is to be used in conjunction with, and within the framework of, the guidance for development of survivor eligibility provided by the Federal (EEOICPA) Procedure Manual.

Section I provides information to help claims examiners identify when a common-law marriage issue exists in an EEOICPA claim. Section II lays out the statutory provisions effecting common-law marriage claims. Section III identifies those states and other jurisdictions which recognize common-law marriages and identifies and explains the five standard elements required to establish a common-law marriage. Sections IV and V provide guidance on developing the evidence necessary to adjudicate the issue of whether a common-law marriage was established. Appendix A sets forth relevant laws of the 18 jurisdictions that currently recognize—or, up until recently, recognized—the creation of common-law marriages.

I. Identifying the Existence of a Common-Law Marriage Issue

Issues of common-law marriage do not arise in the vast majority of EEOICPA claims, and when they do exist it is not always obvious. Thus, claims examiners need to be aware of the tell-tale signs that a common-law marriage issue is involved in the eligibility determination and should be on the lookout for those signs when developing a EEOICPA claim.

The most common tell-tale signs that a common-law marriage issue may need to be developed include: the claimant makes an outright claim of survivor eligibility based on a common-law marriage or lengthy cohabitation; there is no marriage license or certificate or other proof of a legal marriage; the licensed marriage occurred less than one year prior to the employee's death; evidence in the case file suggests that either the employee or the alleged spouse was divorced or was married multiple times; the claimant asserts that an undocumented marriage was legal under Indian tribal laws; or multiple claimants have filed competing claims. Some claims may have only one of these tell-tale signs while others may have many. And the existence of some of these factors does not necessarily mean that a common-law marriage issue exists or must be developed. But if one or more of these factors is present in a case, the claims examiner should treat it as a sign that a common-law marriage issue may be present and that further development may need to be pursued. If the claim is a survivor claim and one of the additional factors listed above is present, the claims examiner should think about the common-law marriage elements discussed in this handbook and should develop the case with those issues in mind. Each of the tell-tale signs is discussed below.

Table 1. Identifying a Common-Law Marriage Issue: Things to Look For

- An outright assertion of common-law marriage or of lengthy cohabitation as a basis for eligibility

- Lack of a marriage license/certificate

- Last-minute marriage

- Evidence of multiple marriages by the employee or an alleged spouse

- Evidence of a divorce by the employee or an alleged spouse

- A claimed Indian tribal marriage

- Competing claims

An Outright Claim of Common-Law Marriage, or a Claim of Eligibility Based on Lengthy Cohabitation with the Deceased Employee

The most obvious sign that a common-law marriage issue must be developed is where the claimant makes a straightforward assertion, on the Form EE-2 or otherwise, that his/her eligibility is based on a common-law marriage. Similarly, while a claimant may not know whether a common-law marriage was actually established, he/she may simply claim eligibility based on the assertion that lengthy cohabitation may give rise to eligibility for survivor benefits.

In this day and time, it is fairly common knowledge that lengthy cohabitation between consenting adults may lead to a common-law marriage and that certain rights, akin to those accorded to ceremonially married husbands and wives, may flow from that relationship. As will be discussed later in this handbook, that common perception is accurate in many states. Every state that recognizes the creation of a common-law marriage requires some period of cohabitation. Thus, while cohabitation by itself does not establish a common-law marriage, if a claimant asserts eligibility based on cohabitation with the employee, he/she may be eligible and the claim should be developed with principles of common-law marriage foremost in mind.

No Marriage License or Certificate

By far the most common type of EEOICPA claim that involves a common-law marriage issue is where the claimant alleges he/she is the deceased employee's spouse, but there is no documented evidence that a legal marriage occurred (no marriage license or certificate, and no court order recognizing a marital relationship). Usually in these cases, the claimant admits that no licensed ceremony took place and that his/her status as the employee's surviving spouse is based on lengthy cohabitation with the employee, *i.e.*, that they established a common-law marriage in a state that recognizes such marriages. It is also the case that a ceremonial marriage that took place without the required state license may lead to a valid common-law marriage.

The common-law marriage issue may also arise in situations in which the alleged spouse of the employee is not a claimant and may not even be alive. For instance, the claimant may assert that he/she is the deceased employee's stepchild due to the assertion that the claimant's mother established a common-law marriage with the employee before the employee's death. In such a case there will not be a marriage certificate and there may be no living spouse from which to gather direct evidence of the claimed common-law marriage. Additionally, while the existence of the marital relationship is critical to the eligibility determination of the stepchild-claimant in such a case, it need not be established that the marriage lasted for the final 365 days of the employee's life. In other words, the stepchild-claimant does not need to prove that the alleged spouse of the employee is an eligible spouse covered under EEOICPA; rather, he/she need only prove that the marital relationship existed and that he/she is indeed the employee's stepchild as described in the Federal (EEOICPA) Procedure Manual.

A claimant may simply check the "spouse" box on the Form EE-2 and not make mention of the fact that he/she and the employee never secured a marriage license, never had a marriage ceremony, and never had a licensed marriage. So if there is no documented evidence to corroborate an alleged marital relationship, the claims examiner should first attempt to obtain the usual evidence, such as a copy of the marriage certificate. But if no documented proof of a legal marriage is produced, the claims examiner should not simply recommend denial for lack of survivor eligibility; rather, the claims examiner should consider developing the case as a common-law marriage case. As shown in the next paragraph however, the mere existence of a marriage certificate does not always mean that consideration of common-law marriage issues can be set aside.

Last-Minute Marriage

Just because the claimant establishes that he/she and the employee were legally married as of the date of the employee's death does not settle the question of whether he/she is an eligible surviving spouse under EEOICPA, because a legal marriage must be in existence for the entire year immediately preceding the death. So if the claimant's formal marriage took place less than one year before the employee died, and the claimant asserts that they established a common-law marriage before the legal marriage, the claims examiner will have to further develop the claim. The death certificate in the "last-minute marriage" type of case will usually show that the employee was married at the time of his death and had a surviving spouse, but when the claims examiner obtains the marriage certificate, it will show that the legal marriage occurred less than one year prior to the employee's death.

Evidence of Multiple Marriages

If there is evidence in the case file that suggests that either the employee or an alleged spouse was married multiple times, the claims examiner should consider the possibility that issues of common-law marriage may factor into the eligibility determination. For example, in one EEOICPA case, two claimants both asserted that they were the employee's eligible surviving spouse. Claimant A produced a marriage certificate showing that she legally married the employee in Kansas in the 1950's. Claimant B also produced a marriage certificate showing that she legally married the employee in Colorado in the 1970's. Claimant A asserted that she was the employee's sole surviving spouse because she had never divorced the employee and, thus, his marriage to the second wife was illegal and void as a bigamous marriage. Claimant B claimed that the employee's first marriage had been dissolved by court order in the 1960's, and that even if it had not been legally dissolved, the employee thought it had been and, thus, his second marriage was legal. Claimant B also alleged that even if the employee's marriage to Claimant A was not dissolved, she (Claimant B) and the employee had lived together as husband and wife for the last 20 years of his life and had, thus, established a common-law marriage.

Similar to the scenario where two spouse-claimants file competing claims, there have also been cases where a spouse-claimant alleges that she is the employee's surviving spouse via a common-law marriage, but the employee's children from a previous legal marriage file their own claims and assert that no common-law marriage was established between the employee and the spouse-claimant, thus entitling the children to a larger share of EEOICPA benefits. Additionally, if a claimant asserts that he/she is the employee's surviving spouse but there is evidence that he/she was married to a third person before his/her marriage to the employee, the claims examiner should seek evidence to determine whether the first marriage was legally dissolved prior to the marriage to the employee. If it was not, the claimant's eligibility may hinge on whether he/she established a common-law marriage with the employee.

Evidence of Divorce

Evidence of divorce should similarly alert the claims examiner to the possibility of a common-law marriage issue in a claim. For instance, several EEOICPA claimants have asserted that although they were once married to and divorced from the employee, they later reconciled and established a common-law marriage prior to the employee's death. While this may seem like an outright claim of common-law marriage that would be easy to detect, such is not always the case. In one such claim, the claimant simply checked the "spouse" box on her Form EE-2, but the claims examiner noticed that the employee's death certificate listed no surviving spouse and indicated that the employee was divorced as of the date of his death. Only upon further development did the claimant explain that she and the employee had been previously married and divorced, but she asserted that they later reconciled and resumed a husband and wife relationship.

The lesson of this case is that any evidence which suggests that the employee or a purported spouse-claimant was previously divorced or that either had multiple marriages should alert the claims examiner to the possibility of a common-law marriage issue. Follow-up development efforts should be made in these cases. Proper development of evidence of multiple marriages or of divorce may also lead to discovery of additional children (possible eligible survivors), which may in turn lead to production of evidence contrary to the claimed marital relationship.

Indian Tribal Marriage

Many employees at uranium mines and mills located throughout the Colorado Plateau are members of federally recognized Indian tribes. These uranium workers and their survivors often file claims for benefits under section 5 of the Radiation Exposure Compensation Act (RECA).

Several EEOICPA survivor claims have been filed by individuals who claim to have been married to a uranium worker under Indian tribal laws, either via a traditional tribal ceremony or under tribal common law. Sometimes, such common-law marriages have been formally recognized in a ruling issued by a tribal court. Sometimes they have not. In either case, tribal law controls the determination of the existence of the claimed marital relationship and development efforts must be targeted to the critical elements set forth in those laws. Thus, anytime a tribal marriage is given as the basis for a survivor claimant's eligibility, the claims examiner should develop the survivor-eligibility aspect of that claim in the same manner as a common-law marriage claim.

Multiple Claimants Filed Competing Claims

If two claimants allege they are the surviving spouse of the same employee, issues of common-law marriage may control the eligibility determination. Likewise, when children and a purported spouse file claims in a single case, common-law marriage issues may be involved. There are several scenarios under which multiple claimants may claim to be the eligible surviving spouse of the same deceased employee. One of those cases was described above in the discussion of multiple marriages. In another case involving competing spouses, the claimant submitted a Navajo Nation marriage license and evidence of a tribal marriage ceremony and claimed that she and the employee were legally married under Navajo tribal law. Another claimant acknowledged that she and the employee did not participate in a tribal marriage ceremony, but claimed that they had earlier established a common-law marriage under Navajo law. In yet another case, there were competing claims filed by a purported surviving spouse and by several children of the deceased employee. The spouse-claimant alleged that she was the employee's third wife and produced documented proof that she and the employee had a legal certified marriage. The employee's children (by his first marriage) claimed that the spouse-claimant was ineligible because her marriage to the employee was invalid due to the fact that the employee had not yet divorced his second wife at the time he married the spouse-claimant. This case involved a determination of whether the spouse-claimant had established a common-law marriage with the employee, even if their legal marriage was invalid due to lack of dissolution of the second marriage. All of these cases are good examples of the complex factual scenarios that sometimes exist in claims involving common-law marriage issues.

Conclusion

It is important for claims examiners to be aware of warning signs of a common-law marriage and to know the various types of claims that may contain issues of common-law marriage. Further development—specifically targeted to the elements of common-law marriage—is almost always necessary in these cases and the guidelines in this handbook should inform that development. Anytime there is evidence (or a lack of evidence) that casts doubt on a person's asserted marital relationship with the employee, further development should be performed with principles of common-law marriage in mind.

II. EEOICPA Provisions Affecting Common-Law Marriage Claims

Surviving Spouse Eligibility

Both Part B and Part E of EEOICPA provide that where a covered employee is deceased at the time EEOICPA benefits are to be paid, payment is to be made to the employee's eligible surviving spouse if such person is living. Under such circumstances, the eligible surviving spouse has priority over all other potentially eligible survivors of the deceased employee and receives EEOICPA benefits to the exclusion of all others, unless there are certain types of children of the employee that are not also children of the spouse (this exception is not addressed in this handbook).

An eligible surviving spouse receives benefits to the exclusion of all others (almost)

While Part B refers to a surviving spouse as a "spouse" and Part E refers to that same person as a "covered spouse," this difference is of no importance in the development of the claim. Both Parts define a "spouse" as a person who was married to the employee for at least one year immediately before the employee's death. DEEOIC is therefore obligated to determine whether such marital relationships exist in order to properly adjudicate EEOICPA claims.

To be eligible for surviving spouse benefits under Part B or Part E, the claimant must have been married to the employee for at least the full year immediately preceding the employee's death

Because EEOICPA does not define key statutory terms such as "wife," "husband," or "married," DEEOIC must look to state law to determine whether a marital relationship exists. If the employee and the claimant secured a marriage license and were united in marriage under the statutory laws of a state and there is no law that invalidates or prohibits their marriage, their marriage will be recognized under federal law. Similarly, if the employee and claimant established a common-law marriage in a state that allows such relationships to be established and recognizes them as valid, federal law recognizes the marital relationship and treats the couple as man and wife for purposes of applying federal laws. Also, state and federal courts have consistently ruled that federally-recognized Indian tribes retain certain inherent powers, including the right to regulate domestic relations among their members. The bottom line is that if state law or the tribal law of a federally-recognized Indian tribe would recognize the existence of a marital relationship, that relationship must be recognized by DEEOIC in its adjudication of EEOICPA survivor claims.

State law (and sometimes Indian tribal law) governs determinations of familial relations

Therefore, where a claimant asserts eligibility as a surviving spouse and the evidence does not sufficiently establish that the claimant had a licensed/certified marriage with the employee for the 365 days immediately prior to the employee's death—or there is some evidence to suggest that the marriage was not valid—the claims examiner may have to gather sufficient evidence to make a determination as to whether the parties established a common-law marriage in a state or other territory which authorizes such marriages. If a legal marriage did occur, but became effective less than a year prior to the employee's death, the claimant must establish that the common-law marriage was established at least a year prior to the employee's death and continued up to the date of the legal marriage. On the other hand, if the legal marriage between the employee and claimant was dissolved in a legal proceeding prior to the employee's death, the claimant must prove that a common-law marriage was established at least a year prior to the employee's death and continued up to the date of the employee's death. In either situation, in order for a spouse-claimant to be eligible under Part B or E, he/she must establish a continuous marital relationship with the employee throughout the entire final year of the employee's life, either through a legal marriage, a common-law marriage, or an uninterrupted combination of the two.

Eligibility of Children, Parents, and Other Survivors

EEOICPA also authorizes survivor benefits for children of deceased employees (and others in Part B only), using a cascading structure of priorities. As announced in EEOICPA Circular No. 08-08 (issued September 23, 2008), for the purposes of adjudicating EEOICPA claims, "a 'child' of an individual under both Parts B and E of EEOICPA can only be a biological child[1], a stepchild, or an adopted child of that individual." Of course, common-law marriage issues may arise in claims filed by child claimants as such claimants may have to prove or disprove the existence of a common-law marriage (of the employee or of their other parent) in order to establish their own eligibility.

The Special Case of RECA Survivors

If a covered uranium employee dies *before* receiving benefits under RECA, his survivors may qualify for the $100,000 award under section 5 of RECA. Under EEOICPA, a person who directly received $100,000 under RECA as the survivor of a covered uranium worker is also entitled to receive $50,000 under Part B, regardless of whether they satisfy the survivorship provisions in EEOICPA. This means that if a purported common-law spouse of a uranium worker received $100,000 from DOJ under section 5 of RECA, that person need not establish that he/she is an eligible spouse under Part B in order to receive Part B benefits. However, if the section 5 awardee (either the uranium worker or such worker's eligible surviving beneficiary as determined by DOJ) is now deceased and an EEOICPA claim is filed by an individual who alleges that he/she contracted a common-law marriage with the deceased section 5 awardee, the usual rules for establishing the alleged common-law marriage will apply.

Survivors who receive RECA section 5 awards directly from DOJ need not prove EEOICPA survivor eligibility to get Part B benefits

Part E does not work like Part B in all respects. In order for any survivor of a uranium worker to qualify for survivor benefits under Part E, the person must satisfy all requirements of survivorship under Part E, regardless of whether that person received the RECA section 5 award or not. Thus, even in the event a purported spouse received $50,000 under Part B because he/she received the section 5 award, that person may not be a "covered spouse" under Part E and must provide sufficient evidence of his/her eligibility as a "covered spouse" in order to receive Part E benefits.

RECA survivor claimants must always prove survivor eligibility to get Part E benefits

Conclusion

To be eligible, a surviving spouse must have been married to the employee for at least the 365 days immediately preceding the covered employee's death. If such spouse is alive at the time EEOICPA benefits are to be paid, he/she is entitled to benefits to the exclusion of almost all other "heirs" of the deceased employee. Thus, because of the priority-based structure of the survivorship provisions of Part B and Part E, the eligibility of every type of survivor—spouse, children, parents, grandchildren, and grandparents—hinges first and foremost on the existence and eligibility of a surviving spouse. If a claimant claims to be a surviving spouse and proves it, then other survivors of the employee will not be eligible (subject to the exception described above). If a claimant alleges that he/she is the surviving child, parent, grandchild, or grandparent of a deceased covered employee, he/she must first prove that there is no eligible surviving spouse. Accordingly, under both Parts B and E, where a survivor claim has been filed and it is established that the covered employee is deceased, the first determination to be made is whether there exists an eligible surviving spouse. And, depending on the evidence presented, that surviving-spouse determination may turn on whether a common-law marriage was established.

All survivor claims hinge on the existence and eligibility of a surviving spouse

III. The State Laws Governing Common-Law Marriage

EEOICPA is a federal law and, thus, its interpretation and application is subject to review by the federal courts, not state courts. However, as has been mentioned, since the statute itself does not include definitions of the operative terms dealing with the marital relationship of a deceased covered employee and his surviving spouse, state law is dispositive of that issue. Also, under certain circumstances, Indian tribal laws control the determination of whether a couple is considered to be married.

In most surviving spouse claims filed under EEOICPA, the evidence of survivor eligibility is clear and uncontradicted. The claimant who alleges to be an eligible surviving spouse of a deceased employee will supply DEEOIC with a copy of a marriage certificate showing that he/she was legally married to the employee in a licensed/certified marriage on a certain date that is at least one year prior to the employee's death. The employee's death certificate will report that the employee was married when he died and will identify the claimant as the employee's surviving spouse. However, the evidence of survivor eligibility is not always quite so crisp and direct and must be further developed to determine if a common-law marriage has been established. As a result, claims examiners must be familiar with the following descriptions of state and tribal laws and must know the critical elements necessary to prove the existence of a common-law marriage.

Common-Law Jurisdictions

Eleven states recognize common-law marriages currently being established within their borders. They are Alabama, Colorado, Iowa, Kansas, Montana, New Hampshire, Oklahoma, Rhode Island, South Carolina, Texas and Utah. In addition to these states, the District of Columbia and at least two federally-recognized Indian tribes—the Navajo Nation and the Pueblo of Acoma—also recognize common-law marriages.[2] Further, four states—Georgia, Ohio, Idaho and Pennsylvania—have recently abolished common-law marriage in their jurisdictions, but will recognize common-law marriages that were created within their borders prior to the date of abolition, so their requirements for contracting a common-law marriage remain relevant.[3] The relevant statutory provisions and case law of these 18 common-law jurisdictions are set forth in Appendix A of this handbook.[4]

While a common-law marriage cannot currently be established in 39 states, all 50 states generally recognize common-law marriages that were

Table 2. The Current Common-Law Marriage States

Alabama • Colorado • Iowa • Utah • Montana • New Hampshire • Texas • Oklahoma • Rhode Island • Kansas • South Carolina

Table 3. Other Common-Law Marriage Jurisdictions

- District of Columbia
- Navajo Nation Tribe
- Pueblo of Acoma Tribe
- Georgia (before 1/2/97)
- Idaho (before 1/1/96)
- Ohio (before 10/10/91)
- Pennsylvania (before 1/2/2005)

validly established in a common-law jurisdiction by persons who were then domiciled in the common-law jurisdiction but later moved into the non-common-law state.[5] The bottom line is that a common-law marriage must be established in one of the few jurisdictions that allow the creation of such marriages, or it is not valid in any jurisdiction, but once a common-law marriage is duly established in a common-law jurisdiction, it will almost always be recognized in any other state.

Choice of Law

Once it is determined that a case may involve a common-law marriage issue, the first questions to answer are in what state (or other jurisdiction) was it allegedly entered into, and did that state (or other jurisdiction) authorize the creation of such marriages within its borders. If full development of the claim results in evidence that the alleged common-law marriage occurred in a state that does not allow the creation of such marriages within its borders—and no other state is involved—then the inquiry may end there. If, on the other hand, the evidence suggests that the parties relocated from state to state during decades of their relationship and one or more of those states is a common-law marriage state, the question of which state's law should be applied to determine the claimant's status as the employee's surviving spouse is not such an easy one to answer and will usually call for further development.

The determination of which state's law applies to the case is critical and the domicile of the parties plays an important role in that determination

EEOICPA does not identify the appropriate state law to be applied in determining the validity of a marriage; thus, a threshold element which must be established in a claim involving a common-law marriage issue is whether the employee and the purported spouse had a sufficient connection to a state that might recognize the claimed common-law marriage. If it can be shown that a common-law marriage was validly established in a state that allows such marriages, DEEOIC will accept that the couple was married for the period of time established by the evidence.

As a general rule, the validity of a marriage is determined by the local law of the state that has "the most significant relationship" to the parties and to the purported marriage.[6] The question as to which state has the most significant relationship to the parties and the marriage is usually answered by looking to the expectations of the parties and to the state with the dominant interest in the matter.[7] The parties would usually expect that the validity of their marriage would be determined by the local law of the state where it was contracted. And the state with the dominant interest is ordinarily the state where the parties were domiciled during the time they claim to have been married.[8]

With regard to common-law marriages, the general rule is that if the parties were domiciled in a state that recognizes common-law marriage and the elements of a common-law marriage were established in that state, the marriage is valid and the parties are spouses for the purposes of EEOICPA. If the state where the parties were domiciled does not recognize common-law marriages, but the claimant alleges to have contracted a valid marriage in another state that does recognize common-law marriage, then the marriage may still be valid, unless the domicile state has a strong public policy against common-law marriages and refuses to recognize them under such circumstances.[9]

The Five Standard Elements of a Common-Law Marriage

There are five elements that are universally applied to the determination of whether a common-law marriage has been entered into; those elements are identified and defined in Table 4 and are: capacity, agreement, cohabitation, holding out, and reputation. Courts in the common-law states do not all employ the same exact calculus in determining whether a common-law marriage has been created within their respective borders, but they do weigh the evidence in terms of these five basic factors in making these decisions. Some states use different terminology and some states couple various factors together and treat them as one. A few of the common-law marriage states hold that proof of one or more of these elements may give rise to a presumption that other of the five elements exist. Whichever of the common-law marriage states is involved, however, evidence of these five basis factors will need to be developed in order to make the eligibility determination.

Table 4. The Standard Elements of a Common-Law Marriage

Capacity—Each of the parties must have the legal capacity to enter into a marriage, *i.e.*, they must each have the capacity to consent (minimum age and mental capacity) and they must each be free of marital ties to any other person.

Agreement—Both parties must mutually intend, consent, and agree to have a present, immediate, and permanent marital relationship with each other.

Cohabitation—The parties must live together openly and continuously as husband and wife and must openly assume the duties and obligations of marriage.

Holding Out—The parties must openly represent to the community that they are husband and wife and must hold themselves out as a married couple.

Reputation—The reputation in the general community must be that the parties are husband and wife.

Capacity

There are several issues that may affect the capacity of a person to enter into a marriage with another person, and capacity requirements are generally applied similarly for both common-law marriages and licensed marriages. Depending on the state, the issues relating to capacity of a person to marry may include age, sex, consanguinity (degree of relation), whether a prior marriage has not yet been dissolved, and mental capacity. The most common capacity issues and those most likely to arise in EEOICPA claims deal with age and prior marriages. In the less likely event that an EEOICPA claim involves a claimed common-law marriage between parties of close relations (*e.g.*, first cousins), or there is a claim of diminished mental capacity of one of the parties, the claims examiner should discuss development with their District Director who may decide to seek early direction from the Solicitor's Office regarding the applicable state law.

Most common-law marriage states have specified a minimum age below which a person is deemed not to have the capacity to enter into a common-law marriage. In Kansas, for instance, both parties must be at least 18 years of age to establish a valid common-law marriage.[10] In Colorado, common-law marriages established on or after September 1, 2006 are only valid if each party is at least 18 years old, although the parties may be as young as 16 if they have parental consent or judicial approval.[11] South Carolina allows common-law marriages between persons as young as 16.[12] States that do not have a statutory age requirement for common-law marriages may apply either the well-recognized common-law ages for marital consent (12 for girls, 14 for boys) or they may apply the ages listed in the state's licensing requirements for licensed marriages (generally 18, unless parental consent is given for those younger).[13] And some states treat marriages involving a party less than the minimum age as void while others treat them as merely voidable. Generally, where the claimed common-law marriage involves a party who was less than 18 years old at the time it was contracted, the claims examiner should fully develop the evidence of age and parental consent along with the evidence regarding the balance of the required elements.

All common-law states have a minimum age requirement for common-law marriages

The common-law marriage states also prohibit the creation of a common-law marriage if one or both of the parties remains married to a third party.[14] The principal is straightforward: plural marriages are prohibited and an existing marriage is an impediment to the formation of a new marriage in every American jurisdiction.[15] Thus, a man cannot enter into a common-law marriage with a woman if he has not yet extinguished the marriage he has with another woman, either through death, divorce or annulment. Likewise, a party may not enter into a licensed marriage if she previously contracted a common-law marriage and did not extinguish that previous marriage by death, divorce, or annulment prior to the licensed marriage. Anytime there is evidence of multiple marriages or multiple cohabitations, either by the deceased employee or the purported common-law spouse, the claims examiner should target development efforts toward uncovering the nature and extent of any relationships that may serve as a legal impediment to the capacity of a party to enter into the claimed common-law marriage, or that may have been an impediment to a claimed licensed marriage. If the existence of a divorce is at issue, for instance, the claims examiner must make all reasonable efforts to obtain a copy of the decree of divorce from the appropriate state court.

All common-law states also prohibit plural marriages, thus a party has to be single to create a common-law marriage

Finally, for claimed Indian tribal marriages, the capacity requirements include membership in the tribe. For instance, membership in the Navajo Tribe is a requirement of a common-law marriage under the Navajo Nation Code and tribal membership must be proven, else the party will not have established the capacity to enter into a common-law marriage under that law.[16]

Agreement

The element of agreement requires that both parties mutually intend, consent and agree to have a present, immediate and permanent marital relationship with each other. All common-law jurisdictions emphasize that the mutual agreement of the parties must be a *present* agreement to *immediately be* husband and wife, not a promise or an agreement that they will get married at some time in the future.[17] The common-law states also consistently require evidence that *both* parties intended and agreed to the immediate and permanent status as husband and wife. For purposes of proof, however, the declared intent of the surviving party to establish an immediate common-law marriage may be coupled with the actions and conduct of the deceased party that are consistent with that intent.[18] However, if the purported spouse asserts that he/she considered herself to be married to the employee, but there is probative evidence showing that the employee did *not* intend or agree to such a relationship, the claims examiner should develop this element further and should specifically ask the claimant for affirmative evidence that the employee intended and agreed to be his/her common-law spouse.

The parties must mutually agree to immediately be husband and wife; a promise to do so in the future is not sufficient to establish a common-law marriage

It is generally understood among common-law states that the parties will not have documented evidence of a past written agreement that clearly pronounced that the parties would go henceforth as husband and wife, particularly where several years have gone by and one of the parties is deceased. All common-law jurisdictions allow the element of agreement to be proven by either words or conduct and hold that it need not be directly proven through production of a written contract or letter evidencing such an agreement.[19] Thus, the states treat this requirement as being one of *implied* agreement and they often look to the cumulate evidence of the other four elements as establishing the requisite agreement. Most common-law jurisdictions hold that evidence of cohabitation may be used as circumstantial evidence of the required mutual agreement, to a greater or lesser extent, but they also clarify that such evidence will not, by itself, constitute sufficient evidence of a common-law marriage.[20]

Evidence of implied consent is sufficient to prove this element

Cohabitation

The element of cohabitation requires that the couple live together openly and continuously *as husband and wife*; merely residing together under the same roof is not sufficient to meet the cohabitation requirement. The character of the cohabitation must be such that it shows that the parties mutually and voluntarily assumed the rights, duties and obligations of marriage, not that they merely lived together and/or had sexual relations.[21] Only one state, New Hampshire, sets a minimum span of time during which the couple must cohabitate in order to satisfy the element of cohabitation.[22] All common-law states, however, require that the cohabitation be open and continuous.[23] For instance, if the parties secretly sleep together or periodically stay overnight at one another's homes, the cohabitation element will not be met.[24] At least two states have required "an exclusive relationship" as part of their analysis of the cohabitation element.[25] Finally, the

Merely living together does not establish the cohabitation element; the couple must live together as husband and wife and assume the duties and obligations of marriage

required cohabitation, like the other elements, must take place in a jurisdiction that recognizes common-law marriage.[26] Cohabitation in a state that does not recognize common-law marriage cannot be used to establish this element.[27] Thus, cohabitation in Missouri (a state that does not allow common-law marriages to be established within its borders) cannot be used to establish a common-law marriage in nearby Kansas (which does allow common-law marriages to be established within its borders).

Holding Out

All common-law states also require that the parties openly hold themselves out in their community as husband and wife.[28] The couple must have "represented to others that they were married."[29] Iowa requires that the parties make "general and public declarations that the parties are husband and wife."[30] Public declarations that the woman is a "girlfriend," "better half," "boss lady," or "housekeeper," are not sufficient and an "isolated statement" that a woman is a man's "wife" has been found not to be sufficient to meet the holding out requirement.[31] The fact that a woman does not use a man's last name weighs against an alleged common-law marriage as it undermines the holding-out requirement.[32] But many states have found that a common-law marriage was established in spite of the woman's occasional or even continuous use of her maiden name.[33]

Like the agreement element, the holding-out element may be proven by either documents or spoken words, or by the conduct and actions of the parties.[34] A secret relationship known only to family or a few friends does not constitute a common-law marriage and occasional introductions as husband and wife do not establish the element of holding out.[35] At least one of the common-law states, Iowa, holds that continuous cohabitation, coupled with holding out in public as husband and wife, creates a presumption of common-law marriage.[36]

Reputation

Finally, the fifth element requires that the evidence establish the existence of a general reputation in the community that the couple is living together as husband and wife, not just having sexual relations and not just residing together for some other mutual convenience. The fact that the relationship is a marriage must be widely known in the community in which the couple lives.[37] There is no such thing as a secret or clandestine common-law marriage.[38] The couple "must so live as to gain the recognition of the public that they are living as man and wife rather than in a state of concubinage."[39]

The parties' reputation as man and wife need not be known to all. Reputation has been described as the understanding among the neighbors and acquaintances with whom the parties associate in their daily life, that they are living together as husband and wife.[40] But, if the couple's reputation in the community is divided or is substantially contradicted, the purported common-law marriage may be found not to exist.[41] Additionally, many of the common-law states hold that open cohabitation, coupled with a reputation in the community as being married, raises a rebuttable presumption that a common-law marriage was created.[42]

Conclusion

State law controls the determination of whether a marital relationship exists between two people and the domicile of the parties usually dictates which state's law applies. Only eleven states currently authorize the creation of common-law marriages within their borders (Alabama, Colorado, Iowa, Kansas, Montana, New Hampshire, Oklahoma, Rhode Island, Texas, South Carolina, and Utah). Almost all states, however, will recognize as valid a common-law marriage created in one of the common-law states. And some states that recently abolished common-law marriage still recognize those marriages established within their boundaries prior to the abolition date.

In order to properly develop the evidence of survivor eligibility in a common-law marriage case, it helps to know the elements that the evidence must prove. The five elements relevant to any determination of a common-law marriage are: capacity, agreement, cohabitation, holding out, and reputation. While the states (and sometimes different courts within the same state) may differ slightly on the weight given to each of these factors, most common-law jurisdictions require proof of each of these elements.

IV. Developing a Common-Law Marriage Issue in an EEOICPA Claim

This section of the handbook provides guidance for claims examiners in their development of the common-law marriage aspect of EEOICPA claims.

As with most EEOICPA claims, further development efforts will be required in common-law claims after the initial submission of supporting evidence. Prior to proceeding with this development, it is important that the claims examiner examine and analyze the currently available evidence and—using the knowledge of common-law marriage provided in this handbook—identify the key issues upon which survivor eligibility determination might turn. From this analysis, the claims examiner should distinguish those elements that can be decided on the available evidence from those upon which need further development is needed. Development efforts should be narrowly targeted.

Development letters should simultaneously inform claimants of the sufficiency of the evidence already submitted and ask that they submit evidence to address open issues and weaknesses in their case. EEOICPA regulations require that DEEOIC "notify the claimant of deficiencies and provide him or her an opportunity for correction of the deficiencies."[43] Before the issuance of a recommended decision, development letters serve as the vehicle for that required notice. In common-law marriage cases, the development letter should clearly identify any necessary element of survivor eligibility that the current evidence does not support or for which the current evidence is not adequate to make a determination. The letter should then ask well-tailored questions to elicit new information on those elements. The requests for information should not ask for more than is required. If there is sufficient evidence in the case file to make a determination on the element of capacity, for example, the development letter should not ask for evidence of that element, unless clarification is needed or a contradiction in existing evidence suggests that additional evidence would improve the quality of the decision.

Developing the Two Threshold Issues

Although different common-law claims may require different targeted and customized development efforts, there are certain threshold issues that must be developed in every type of common-law marriage case. The first of these issues is *when* the common-law marriage was entered into, and the second is the place *where* it was entered into.

The two most important aspects of a claimed common-law marriage is when and where it was first established

The initial development letter sent in a common-law marriage case should always request a narrative statement from the claimant fully describing the nature and duration of the marital relationship upon which survivor eligibility is based, including when and where the relationship began. For instance, in the case of a claimant who simply alleges to be a spouse via common-law marriage but has supplied little background information about the relationship, the development

Ask for a sworn statement fully describing the history of the claimed marital relationship

letter should ask that the claimant supply a narrative statement explaining the circumstances surrounding the creation of the common-law marriage, along with other important events in the marriage such as relocations, interruptions in periods of cohabitation, children and divorce. The development letter should also request any available documents that would tend to prove the claimed relationship.

The date on which the common-law marriage was contracted is important for several reasons, the first of which is the date's interplay with EEOICPA's one-year marriage requirement for surviving spouses. If development of the evidence elicits a declaration from the claimant that the alleged common-law marriage was entered into only six months prior to the employee's death, a few well-targeted development questions may quickly establish that the claimant is clearly not eligible since the marital relationship must have been established at least one full year prior to the employee's death. The claimed date of creation of the common-law marriage also sets the point in time at which the parties' domicile should initially be determined. Further, it sets the point in time at which the parties must have the capacity to enter into a common-law marriage; because of this, the parties' ages on that date are important and the fact of whether the parties were each single prior to that date may need to be developed. The establishment date must also fall during a period of time that the domicile state allowed the creation of common-law marriages. As shown above, many states have abolished common-law marriages established within their borders, some fairly recently, but none of these laws have retroactive effect, so if the claimed common-law marriage was validly established prior to the date of abolishment, it will be recognized.

Of similar importance is the *place* where the common-law marriage was allegedly contracted. Because state law controls the common-law marriage determination, a threshold issue in all common-law marriage claims is the determination of which state's law should be applied to the case. For that reason, the claims examiner must fully develop the evidence establishing where each of the parties was domiciled during the entire period of the claimed common-law marriage, particularly on the date the marriage was first established. For example, in one actual EEOICPA case the claimant purported to be the eligible surviving spouse of the deceased employee. She asserted that the common-law marriage occurred in 1978 and that the couple resided in Colorado in 1978 and 1979, then moved to Utah for "about nine years," then moved back to Colorado for an unstated period of time, then moved to Nevada, then returned to Colorado again from 1995 to 1997, then lived in Arizona from 1999 until the employee's 2003 death. Of these four states, only Colorado and Utah allow the creation of common-law marriages; Nevada and Arizona do not. However, the claimant produced no documented evidence to corroborate her claim that the couple was domiciled in Colorado in the 1978-1979 timeframe and she initially produced insufficient evidence of the elements required for a common-law marriage in either Colorado or Utah. In a case such as this one, the claims examiner should further develop the evidence of a domicile in Colorado and Utah (the two common-law states in which the claimant alleged the couple resided as husband and wife), and should develop the evidence of each of the five elements of a common-law marriage in both Colorado and Utah. If the claimant can supply sufficient evidence to support a finding that he/she and the employee established a common-law marriage in either of the common-law states in which they were domiciled, and that that marriage was established at least one year prior to the employee's death and was not dissolved prior to his death, he/she will have met EEOICPA's requirements for a surviving spouse.

As noted in an example above, the evidence must be sufficient to establish that a common-law marriage was established in a common-law state at a time when that state allowed the creation of such marriages. Conversely, the claimant need not prove that he/she and the employee established a common-law marriage in every state in which they resided as husband and wife. Likewise, the claimant is not required to prove that every state in which the couple cohabitated was a common-law state. Meeting the common-law marriage requirements of one common-law state is all that is required, as long as the marriage was established in that state at least one year prior to the employee's death and was not dissolved prior to the employee's death. Developing evidence of locations and time frames where the alleged married couple cohabitated is very important to the determination of eligibility since state law controls whether a marital relationship existed.

So if, for example, a claimant alleges that he/she is a deceased employee's common-law spouse but submits very little supporting evidence, a development letter must be sent to the claimant, informing him/her that additional information is needed before DEEOIC can determine his/her eligibility. The letter should ask that the claimant submit a statement and then instruct him/her as follows:

It is important that your statement include as much information as possible that supports your claim that you and the employee entered into a common-law marriage. Your statement should include a narrative that describes your relationship with the employee and, additionally, provides the following information:

- *The date on which you and the employee entered into a common-law marriage and a description of the surrounding circumstances and why you believe your common-law marriage began on that date.*

- *The state in which you and the employee were domiciled as of the date you provided in response to the above question, and a narrative description of any residential moves or relocations that you and the employee made after that date. Please identify the time frame (start and end dates) during which you and the employee resided together in each location as husband and wife.*

The answers to these "when" and "where" questions play a critical role in the determination of the claimant's eligibility and provide crucial context for the consideration of all other evidence presented. The development letter should not just ask for a narrative statement, it should also request documented evidence to corroborate the narrative assertions and support the claimant's claim of survivor eligibility.

Developing Evidence of the Five Standard Elements of a Common-Law Marriage

As noted above, many of the common-law states treat evidence of one of the five elements as circumstantial evidence of the existence of other elements. Despite this, claims examiners should try to develop evidence of all five elements. Development letters should be designed to elicit sufficient evidence of all five common-law marriage elements, unless there is already sufficient evidence of some of these elements in the file. Claims examiners should be careful not to ask claimants to make efforts to find and submit historical documents to prove a factor that is already sufficiently established by the evidence in the case file, unless clarification is required or conflicting evidence exists.

Below are sample questions designed to elicit evidence of the five standard elements:

> *State the ages of both you and the employee on the date you began your common-law marriage and whether you or the employee had any marital ties to any other person on that date.*
>
> *Identify the state in which you and the employee were domiciled as of the date you began a common-law marriage, and provide a narrative description of all locations where you and the employee lived after that date. For each location, identify the time frame (start and end dates) during which you and the employee lived together as husband and wife.*
>
> *Provide a narrative description of when you and the employee agreed to have a present, immediate and permanent marital relationship as husband and wife, and your description of the timing and circumstances surrounding that agreement.*
>
> *Provide a narrative description of whether you and the employee held yourselves out to the public as husband and wife, and a description of the times, places and surrounding circumstances of such representations.*
>
> *Provide a narrative description of whether you and the employee had a reputation in the general community as being husband and wife and identify any persons submitting affidavits who will describe such a reputation.*

Developing Evidence in a Simple Surviving-Spouse Claim

Imagine the most simple, straightforward common-law marriage claim where the claimant asserts that he/she is the deceased employee's surviving spouse via a common-law marriage, no competing claims have been filed and the evidence proves that neither party was ever married to another person. As simple as this example sounds, such claims come in many varieties, for instance:

- Scenario A: Where the employee and the claimant were never legally married, but the claimant asserts they contracted a common-law marriage.

- Scenario B: Where the employee and the claimant were legally married then divorced, but the claimant asserts that they later reconciled and entered into a common-law marriage prior to the employee's death.

- Scenario C: Where the employee and the claimant entered into a licensed marriage less than a year prior to the employee's death, but the claimant asserts that they established a common-law marriage prior to the licensed marriage.

The primary survivor-eligibility issues that must be determined in each of these three situations differ slightly, but run along the same basic theme; that is, the claimant must prove that he/she and the employee were continuously married for at least the last 365 days of the employee's life (whether by licensed marriage, by common-law marriage, or by a combination of the two).

A continuous marriage for the last year of the employee's life is the key to surviving spouse eligibility

In Scenario A, the primary issues that need to be developed are: (1) was a common-law marriage established between the claimant and the employee; (2) if so, was it established at least one year prior to the employee's death; and (3) if both (1) and (2) are found to be true, was the common-law marriage dissolved prior to the employee's death. In order to make the determinations relating to these three primary issues, the claims examiner needs to develop the two threshold issues of "when" and "where" the claimed common-law marriage was initially established, and needs to develop evidence on each of the five standard elements of a common-law marriage as described previously in this section. In addition, the claims examiner needs to develop evidence to determine if the common-law marriage was ever dissolved and, if so, when.

In Scenario B, the development issues differ from those in Scenario A and are: (1) was a common-law marriage established between the claimant and the employee; (2) if the divorce occurred more than one year prior to the employee's death, was the common-law marriage established at least one year prior to the employee's death and did it continue to the employee's death; and (3) if the divorce was made final during the last year of the employee's life, was there any interruption between the divorce and the creation of the common-law marriage.

In Scenario C, the development issues are similar but again slightly different: (1) was a common-law marriage established between the claimant and the employee; (2) was it established at least one year prior to the employee's death; (3) did the common-law marriage continue up to the date of the licensed marriage; and (4) was the licensed marriage dissolved prior to the date of the employee's death.

As these three examples illustrate, in a common-law marriage case the claims examiner always needs to develop evidence of the two threshold issues of "when" and "where" the claimed common-law marriage was initially established, and needs to develop evidence on each of the five standard elements of a common-law marriage to determine whether a common-law marriage was ever established. The facts of each individual case will then dictate what additional issues need to be developed in order to allow the survivor-eligibility determination to be made.

Developing a Capacity Issue

Development efforts may be far more complex in the case where the claimant alleges to be a surviving spouse but there is some evidence that suggests that the claimed marital relationship doesn't exist because one of the parties lacked the legal capacity to marry. This situation may arise where there are two different claimants, both of whom claim to be the employee's surviving spouse, or it may arise where only one claimant files a claim. The capacity issue may arise in many different circumstances, including, among others:

- Where either the employee or the surviving-spouse claimant was underage at the time the alleged common-law marriage was established.

- Where the employee had a prior legal marriage with another woman/man before he/she entered into the asserted common-law marriage with the claimant, and the prior marriage was not dissolved prior to the date upon which the common-law marriage was alleged to have occurred.

- Where the employee established a common-law marriage with Claimant A before he/she entered into a licensed marriage with Claimant B, and the prior marriage was not dissolved prior to the latter marriage.

- Where the *claimant* had a prior legal marriage with another man/woman before she/he entered into the asserted common-law marriage with the employee, and the prior marriage was not dissolved prior to the date upon which the employee-claimant marriage was alleged to have occurred.

If the main issue of capacity involves the age of the one of the parties, the development of that element is straightforward (*i.e.*, ask for proof of the parties' ages on the date the common-law marriage was established), but the claims examiner may, depending on the state's law, need to develop evidence of parental or judicial consent.

More common is an issue involving whether one of the parties to the claimed common-law marriage was actually free to marry the other. If there is some indirect evidence that this situation may be present (for instance, a passing reference to a previous spouse in a medical record), a generic development question should be used to address the issue; for example:

> *Provide a narrative description of whether you or the employee have been legally married to any other persons, or have children by any other relationship, or have cohabited with another person for a length of time such that a common-law marriage may have been established with that other person. For each such situation, please identify the parties and/or children involved, the places and dates of the marriage, relationship or cohabitation, and the date and manner in which each marriage, relationship or cohabitation was terminated, dissolved or annulled, either by death, court order or otherwise.*

If the file already contains evidence or an allegation that the employee or the claimant was previously married and that that marriage may not have been dissolved, the development questions should be more pointed, for example:

> *You claim that you are the eligible surviving spouse of Mr. Employee by virtue of a common-law marriage that you and he began in Oklahoma two years prior to his death. However, there is evidence in your case file (a marriage certificate) that suggests that you were legally married to another man prior to that time. Please provide a narrative description of your relationship with your prior husband and provide documents to support your description of how and when that relationship ended (e.g., a divorce decree or death certificate).*

Another example might be as follows:

> *You claim to be the eligible surviving spouse of Mr. Employee and have provided a copy of your marriage certificate in support. However, there is evidence in your case file (a marriage certificate) that the employee was married to [insert name here] prior to his marriage to you. Additionally, there is no evidence in the case file that Mr. Employee was ever divorced from [insert name here]. Please provide a narrative description of your understanding of whether Mr. Employee's marriage to [insert name here] was ever dissolved by court order or otherwise and provide documents or other evidence to support your description of how and when that relationship ended (e.g., a divorce decree, death certificate, affidavit from witnesses).*

The development letter in such a complicated case should be targeted narrowly. It should inform the claimant of the nature and extent of the evidence in the case file (or lack thereof) that led to the additional questions and should provide a very specific request for additional evidence. Like all development letters, such a letter should always request documentation to support all aspects of eligibility that the evidence does not yet support. The letter should also make very clear to the claimant the key issue behind the additional request for information and how that issue affects the claimant's eligibility under the Act.

Developing Evidence in a Stepchild Claim

In the context of common-law marriage cases, a stepchild claim is presented when the claimant asserts that he/she is an eligible survivor by virtue of the fact that he/she is the child of a parent who was married to the employee via a common-law marriage and that he/she lived with the employee in a regular parent-child relationship. In such a case, the primary survivor-eligibility issues that must be determined are: (1) did a common-law marriage exist between the claimant's biological parent and the employee; and (2) if so, did the claimant live with the employee in a regular parent-child relationship *during the common-law marriage*.

It is important to note that in the stepchild case, it does not matter whether the common-law marriage between the employee and the claimant's parent endured for at least one year immediately prior to the employee's death, so development need not be targeted to that non-issue. The only "timing" issues that must be developed in such a case are: (1) was the alleged common-law marriage created in a state during a time when that state allowed common-law marriages; and (2) did the claimant live with the employee in a regular parent-child relationship after the common-law marriage had been established and before it was dissolved (if ever). If, for instance, the child-claimant lived with the employee during a time when the employee was merely dating the child-claimant's parent, then the child left for college prior to the creation of the common-law marriage between his/her parent and the employee, the child-claimant is likely not an eligible stepchild. In a stepchild claim where a common-law marriage is alleged, the claims examiner should flesh out evidence of these other details in addition to developing the threshold evidence of "when" and "where" the common-law marriage was established and the five standard elements of such a marriage.

In a stepchild claim, the evidence need not prove a continuous marriage for the last year of the employee's life

Developing Evidence of a Marriage Under Indian Tribal Law

There have been several EEOICPA claims with alleged common-law marriages that involved Indian tribal law. Most such cases have been filed by survivors of uranium workers who received benefits from the Department of Justice under section 5 of RECA. While most of these claims were filed by members of the Navajo Nation Tribe, at least one has been filed by a member of the Pueblo of Acoma Tribe.

The Department of the Interior maintains a list of federally recognized Indian tribes and both the Navajo Nation and the Pueblo of Acoma are on that list.[44] The U.S. Supreme Court has held that federally recognized Indian tribes retain certain inherent powers, including the right "to regulate domestic relations among members."[45] Therefore, a marriage that is valid under the laws of a federally recognized Indian tribe will, generally, qualify as a marriage under federal law, and a party to such a marriage could be eligible as a "spouse" under Part B of EEOICPA and a "covered spouse" under Part E if the marital relationship is proven.

Initially, it should be noted that the domestic relations laws of both the Navajo Nation and the Pueblo of Acoma Tribe only apply when both parties of an alleged tribal marriage are members of the tribe, so the claims examiner should always develop this capacity issue in every tribal marriage case. The development of additional elements depends on law of the tribe at issue. Additionally, the Navajo Nation Code explicitly provides that Navajo "Peacemaker Courts" may enter an order, after the fact, validating a common-law marriage between tribe members.[46] On occasion, such orders have been entered *after* the death of one or both of the parties and such orders are generally accepted as sufficient proof of the existence of a marital relationship.

Tribe membership must always be proven in claims of marriage under Indian tribal laws

In any case in which a claimant asserts that a common-law marriage was created under Navajo tribal law, the claims examiner should develop the two threshold issues of "when" and "where" and the five standard elements of a common-law marriage and should, additionally, inquire as to whether an order (often referred to as a "Peacemaking Judgment") has been entered by the Navajo Courts validating the alleged marriage.

The domestic relations laws of the Pueblo of Acoma Tribe differ significantly from those of the Navajo Nation Tribe. The Pueblo of Acoma Laws (2003) simply state that marriage involving members of their Tribe "shall be recognized if performed according to the laws of the state of their residence or according to tribal custom."[47] Those laws also state that "[r]ecognition of a marriage by the Pueblo of Acoma will be shown on a certificate of marriage" and that a "marriage registry shall be maintained in the Acoma Tribal Offices."[48] Thus, in a Pueblo of Acoma case, the claims examiner should develop the issue of capacity (including tribe membership) and also whether there is a "certificate of marriage" and a written entry in the "marriage registry" maintained by the offices of the Tribal Court. If either the certificate or registry entry exists, it may not be necessary to develop the five standard elements of a common-law marriage depending on the circumstances of the case, *i.e.*, if the evidence of the timing of the marriage is sufficient to establish survivor eligibility in the particular case.

Documents & Supporting Evidence

Development letters should not only ask for written statements of certain facts but, as has been repeated throughout this handbook, should also always request that the claimant submit pertinent documents to corroborate and support any factual claim relating to survivor eligibility. The regulations explicitly address the evidentiary limitations of written statements and the need for documented evidence:

Narrative assertions of common-law marriage, unsupported by documented evidence, are usually not sufficient to satisfy the claimant's burden of proof

> Written affidavits or declarations, subject to penalty of perjury, by the employee, survivor or any other person, will be accepted as evidence of. . .survivor relationship for purposes of establishing eligibility and may be relied on in determining whether a claim meets the requirements of the Act for benefits if, and only if, such person attests that due diligence was used to obtain records in support of the claim, but that no records exist.

20 C.F.R. § 30.111(c). The "if, and only if" language makes very clear that mere written statements (even those that are notarized) cannot be used to establish elements of survivor eligibility unless either supporting documents ("records") are submitted or the written statement contains the attestation required by the regulation.

Depending on the situation and the extent of documented evidence of eligibility already submitted, the claims examiner may want to provide the claimant with a list of examples of the types of documents that might support eligibility. For example, a development letter may include a statement similar to the following:

> *In addition to the narrative description provided in your statement, please provide proof to support the factual assertions in your statement. Be aware that the time frame of events is important, so documents that are dated may be particularly helpful to your claim. Also, make sure to address dates and time frames in any affidavit you submit. In the event no records exist to support your assertions, include in your affidavit a statement that you have used due diligence in an attempt to obtain supporting records but that no such records exist. Listed below are examples of types of documents that may include information supportive of a claim of common law-marriage:*
>
> • *Affidavits—Affidavits are signed, narrative statements submitted by you or any other person who has personal knowledge of the information included in statement itself. You should submit a written affidavit describing the basis of your claim to be the employee's common-law spouse, as described above. You may want to ask other people to prepare affidavits also if you think others may have relevant information to provide. You can submit their affidavits to us along with your own, or the persons making the*

affidavit may submit them to our office directly. Any submission to our office needs to clearly show your case number.

- *Marriage & Divorce Documents—Marriage licenses and certificates may provide information relevant to your status as a common-law spouse. Also, if you or the employee were married to other persons, you should submit marriage certificates and dissolution decrees regarding those other marriages. You should also submit any declaratory judgments or court orders which officially recognize the claimed marriage between you and the employee.*

- *Other Court Documents—If you and the employee ever filed a civil lawsuit regarding the employee's occupational exposure, or were involved in any other type of court action or workers' compensation claim, documents from such cases may include information relevant to your common-law marriage claim.*

- *Death Certificates—The employee's death certificate may supply information relevant to your common-law marriage claim. Additionally, if you or the employee was a widow or widower at the time of your common-law marriage to each other, you may want to submit the death certificate of the former spouse.*

- *Children's Records—Birth or death certificates of any children which you and the employee had together may provide relevant evidence of your relationship with the employee.*

- *Real Estate Documents—Deeds and rental/lease agreements may provide relevant information.*

- *Tax Documents—Federal and state tax returns may supply relevant information to your common-law marriage claim.*

- *Banking & Loan Documents—Relevant information may be found in dated statements from checking and savings accounts, car loan documents, promissory notes, security agreements, and mortgage documents.*

- *Contracts or Insurance Documents—Any written contract or other standard insurance document may include information relevant to your claim as being the employee's common-law spouse.*

- *Employment Documents—Employment documents, such as beneficiary designation forms for employer-provided life insurance or health insurance applications, may include information that is relevant to your common-law marriage claim.*

- *Medical Records—Hospital records may contain relevant information.*

- *Vehicle Registration Documents—If you and the employee owned any vehicles together, licensure and registration documents may show relevant information.*

- *Tribal Documents—If you and the employee are members of an Indian tribe and you claim a common-law marriage under tribal law, you should submit documents from the tribal records that show membership and any tribal court declarations concerning your claimed relationship.*

- *Wills, Trusts, and Power of Attorney Documents—Testamentary documents such as wills and trusts may include information relevant to your claim to be the employee's common-law spouse.*

- *Utility Bills—Utility bills mailed to you and the employee may reveal relevant information.*

- *Letters—Letters in which you and the employee referred to each other as husband and wife may be relevant to your claimed status. Also, letters from or to others that refer to your relationship with the employee may be relevant.*

- *Other Documents—You should submit any other formal or informal documents that may support your claim to be the employee's common-law spouse. For instance, any document which shows your use of the employee's last name as your own last name, or that shows that your children from another marriage used the employee's last name as their last name would be relevant. Also any form that the employee ever completed wherein you were listed as spouse would be relevant.*

Conclusion

Development letters should always inform the claimant of any deficiencies in the evidence and should include well-tailored questions designed to elicit sufficient information to support findings regarding each element of survivor eligibility. In common-law marriage claims, claims examiners should always develop evidence of the two threshold issues of "when" and "where" the common-law marriage started. Development letters in such cases should also seek probative evidence of each of the five elements of a common-law marriage: capacity, agreement, cohabitation, holding out, and reputation. The nature of the claim and the asserted status of the claimant involved will dictate the determining factors in a common-law marriage claim but, generally speaking, a spouse-claimant is required to prove that he/she and the employee were continuously married for the last year of the employee's life, whether by licensed marriage, common-law marriage, or an uninterrupted combination of the two. These basic factors drive the analysis and development efforts in most common-law marriage claims. The regulations require survivor claimants to exercise due diligence in gathering documented evidence to support their eligibility and development letters in such cases should specifically request both a narrative statement and corroborating documents.

V. Other Issues Affecting Development of Common-Law Marriage Claims

Submitting the Claim to the National Office

Once all development efforts are completed in a claim involving a common-law marriage issue, the case file should be forwarded to the Policy Branch for guidance pursuant to the Federal (EEOICPA) Procedure Manual.[49] The claim should *not* be sent to the National Office until the case has been fully and adequately developed consistent with the guidance in this handbook.

The regulations place the burden on claimants to produce all evidence necessary to establish their eligibility to EEOICPA benefits.[50] Similarly, the regulations require survivor-claimants to exercise due diligence in gathering evidence to support their eligibility in any type of case, including claims of survivor eligibility based on a claimed common-law marriage.[51] If a claimant is responding to ongoing development efforts, the claims examiner should continue to develop any common-law marriage issues until sufficient evidence to support a determination of eligibility has been gathered. If the claimant repeatedly fails to respond to development letters sent to the claimant's confirmed residence address, the claims examiner should note that fact in the case file and seek guidance from the District Director on whether the case is ripe to be sent to the National Office for review, or whether additional efforts should be made to gather further evidence before submission to the National Office.

The Burden of Proof

In addition to their burden of production, the regulations also provide that claimants carry the burden of proof on each element of their eligibility for EEOICPA benefits.[52] Thus, if a claimant asserts that he/she is the surviving spouse of a deceased covered employee via a common-law marriage, it is the claimant's burden to prove that a valid common-law marriage was created. On the other hand, if a claimant's eligibility depends on the invalidity of a common-law marriage, the burden of proof falls on the claimant alleging the invalidity of the marriage. For example, if a child-claimant asserts that he/she is the sole eligible survivor of a deceased covered employee because there is no living and eligible surviving spouse, he/she carries the burden to prove that there is no eligible surviving spouse, which may require proof that there was no valid common-law marriage between the employee and a third party who claims to be a surviving spouse.

In certain circumstances, legal presumptions work to shift the burden of proof and, in the context of EEOICPA claims, may work to effectively reduce the number of elements that a claimant must prove in order to establish eligibility. For example, Pennsylvania law recognizes a rebuttable presumption of common-law marriage when only the two elements of cohabitation and reputation are established.[53] Thus, if the claimant establishes that he/she and the employee cohabitated and were domiciled in Pennsylvania prior to January 2, 2005 (the date after which no common-law marriage can be established in that state), and they had a reputation in their community as being husband and wife, it is presumed that they contracted a common-law marriage. The burden then shifts to a competing claimant, if there is one, to prove that the marriage was not validly established. If there is no competing claimant but probative evidence exists that contradicts the existence of one of the required elements, that contradictory evidence may rebut the presumption and support a finding against the claimed common-law marriage. Other states also recognize such rebuttable presumptions in favor of marriage.[54] Although such presumptions may ultimately reduce the elements necessary for eligibility, claims examiners should develop all of the five standard elements of a common-law marriage prior to submitting the claim file to the Policy Branch for review.

The Character and Weight of Evidence

In developing an EEOICPA claim, it should be understood that it is well-established among common-law states that circumstantial evidence may be relied upon to demonstrate a common-law marriage.[55]

There are basically two kinds of evidence, direct evidence and circumstantial evidence. Direct evidence is evidence based on personal knowledge or observation and that, if true, proves a fact without resort to inference or presumption. If a claimant's long-time neighbor submits a notarized affidavit attesting that the claimant and the covered employee publicly declared to that neighbor several times during the last 10 years that they were husband and wife, that statement is direct evidence of the element of holding out. Circumstantial evidence, on the other hand, is generally described as evidence based on inference and not on personal knowledge or observation; that is, it is evidence of minor facts or circumstances from which the existence of or nonexistence of a fact at issue may be inferred.[56] If the claimant's sister who lives in California attests that the claimant and the deceased covered employee had uninterrupted cohabitation in Maryland for the last two years of the employee's life, and her basis of knowledge is that she visited them twice during that period of time, her statement is circumstantial evidence, not direct evidence, of the asserted period of cohabitation.

While direct proof of a fact is generally considered the most probative and compelling evidence of that fact, claimants are not required by either state law, or the EEOICPA statute or regulations, to provide direct proof of every element of a claimed common-law marriage. Thus, a claimed common-law marriage should not be denied simply for lack of direct evidence of one of the required elements, if probative evidence of the other elements has been produced and the missing element is supported by circumstantial evidence. And, while development efforts should seek direct evidence of the required elements of a common-law marriage, they should inform claimants that any proof that tends to support their claimed eligibility will be received and considered.

Finally, contradictions in evidence do not preclude a finding that a common-law marriage was created. Contradictions and inconsistencies in evidence go to the weight and probative value to be given individual pieces of evidence by the fact finder; their mere existence does not require a finding of insufficiency of the evidence on any particular element of eligibility. If, for example, the employee's death certificate reports that the employee was widowed at the time of his death, but sworn affidavits of disinterested witnesses are submitted and sufficiently establish that the employee was in a common-law marriage at the time of his death, the documented evidence in the death certificate may be outweighed by the witnesses' statements. Depending on the character and source of information, it may be reasonable to assign greater weight to certain evidence even if it is contradicted by other, albeit less probative, information.

Conclusion

Claimants in EEOICPA cases are assigned the burden to produce all necessary evidence and to establish each element of their eligibility by a preponderance of the evidence. Once development efforts have been completed in a case that includes a common-law marriage issue, the case file is to be forwarded to the Policy Branch for review and guidance on whether the evidence is sufficient to establish the claimed common-law marriage under state law. Additionally, circumstantial evidence may be sufficient to support a claim of common-law marriage, so development efforts need not necessarily be prolonged while awaiting direct evidence of every single element. Finally, it is important to note that contradictions in evidence go to the weight given to certain evidence and do not, by their mere existence, dictate a finding that the evidence of a common-law marriage is insufficient.

The purpose of development regarding a claimed common-law marriage is to obtain sufficient information and probative evidence to support a determination regarding whether a common-law marriage was ever created and, if so, its duration. If those two things can be decided, then the impact of the common-law marriage on the eligibility of all affected claimants can be determined. If those two things cannot be determined from the evidence submitted, then either additional development needs to be performed or a decision must be made that the claimant has failed to satisfy his/her burden of production and proof because the evidence is insufficient to prove the claimant's eligibility. In the former case, the development efforts should be narrowly tailored to obtain the evidence that is needed to make the factual determinations critical to eligibility. In the latter case, the claims examiner should recommend that the claim be denied.

Endnotes

[1] "Biological" children include ALL biological immediate descendants: those who are legitimate children; illegitimate (referred to in the statute as "natural") children, regardless of whether or not they were "recognized" by the employee during his lifetime; and children born after the death of the employee.

[2] The two Indian tribes mentioned only recognize marriages established between registered members of their respective tribes. The Navajo Nation is situated within the exterior boundaries of Arizona, New Mexico and Utah; thus, common-law marriage claims dealing with Navajo tribal law generally arise in claims involving those states. The Pueblo of Acoma tribal boundaries are located entirely within the state of New Mexico.

[3] Pennsylvania continues to recognize common-law marriages created before January 2, 2005; Georgia, those created before January 2, 1997; Idaho, those created before January 1, 1996; and Ohio, those created before October 10, 1991.

[4] In addition to the eighteen common-law jurisdictions addressed in detail by this handbook, twelve other states abolished common-law marriage between 1920 and 1968 and still recognize such marriages created prior to their respective dates of abolition. Those states and their date of abolition are as follows (common-law marriages created prior to the dates shown will be recognized as valid): Florida (December 1, 1968), Hawaii (April 6, 1920), Indiana (January 2, 1958), Michigan (January 2, 1957), Minnesota (April 27, 1941), Mississippi (April 6, 1956), Missouri (April 1, 1921), Nebraska (August 2, 1923), Nevada (March 30, 1943), New Jersey (December 2, 1939), New York (April 29, 1933), and South Dakota (July 1, 1959). Any claimed common-law marriage in those states prior to the abolition date should be fully developed using the guidance in this handbook and the Solicitor's Office will then research the state law and provide an opinion on a case-by-case basis.

[5] *See, e.g., Knight v. Superior Court*, 128 Cal.App.4th 14, 19-20, 26 Cal.Rptr.3d 687, 690-691 (Cal. App. 3 Dist. 2005); *Craig v. Carrigo*, 121 S.W.3d 154, 160 (Ark. 2003); *Estate of Lamb*, 655 P.2d 1001, 1002-1003 (N.M. 1982). Additionally, the United States Supreme Court recognizes the validity of common-law marriages, as long as no local statutory provision prohibits their creation. *Meister v. Moore*, 96 U.S. 76, 79 (1877).

[6] *Restatement (Second) Conflicts of Laws* § 283(1) (1971); *United States v. Seay*, 718 F.2d 1279, 1285 & n.10 (4th Cir. 1983).

[7] *Restatement (Second) Conflicts of Laws* § 283, Comment b. on Subsection (1).

[8] *Metropolitan Life Ins. Co. v. Manning*, 568 F.2d 922, 926 (2nd Cir. 1977). Domicile is the place that a person regards as their true, fixed, principal, and

permanent home. It differs from residence, which means the place where one is actually physically present as an inhabitant, in that domicile includes an intention to return and remain even though currently residing elsewhere.

[9] *See e.g., Lynch v. Bowen*, 681 F.Supp. 506 (N.D. Ill. 1988); *Metropolitan Life Ins. Co. v. Chase*, 294 F.2d 500, 503-04 (3rd Cir. 1961).

[10] *See* Kan. Stat. Ann. § 23-101 (2009). Prior to the recent legislation in Kansas, the requisite age for common-law marriage in that state was twelve for girls and fourteen for boys.

[11] *See* Colo. Rev. Stat. Ann. §§ 14-2-104, 14-2-109.5 (2009). Common-law marriages established in Colorado prior to September 2006 may be valid even if the parties are as young as twelve for girls and fourteen for boys. *See In re Marriage of J.M.H. and Rouse*, 143 P.3d 1116, 1119 (Colo.App. 2006) (recognizing a common-law marriage involving a 15-year-old girl).

[12] *See* S.C. Code 1976 § 20-1-200 (2008) (providing that effective June 11, 1997, parties must be at least 16 years old to enter into a common-law marriage in South Carolina).

[13] *See, e.g., Adams v. Boan*, 559 So.2d 1084, 1086-1087 (Ala. 1990); *Teague v. Allred*, 173 P.2d 117, 118-119 (Mont. 1946).

[14] *See, e.g.,* Colo. Rev. Stat. Ann. §§ 14-2-110 (2009) (prohibiting a marriage "entered into prior to the dissolution of an earlier marriage of one of the parties.").

[15] The act of plural marriage is referred to as polygamy, the associated crime is termed bigamy.

[16] *See* 9 N.N.C. §§ 8-9 (1993); *see also United States v. Jarvison*, 409 F.3d 1221, 1225 (10th Cir. 2005).

[17] *See, e.g., Staudenmayer v. Staudenmayer*, 714 A.2d 1016, 1020-1021 (Pa. 1998); *Nestor v. Nestor*, 472 N.E.2d 1091, 1094 (Ohio 1984).

[18] *In re Marriage of Martin*, 681 N.W.2d 612, 617 (Iowa 2004).

[19] *See, e.g., Wilkins v. Wilkins*, 48 P.3d 644, 649 (Idaho 2002); *Matter of Estate of Hunsaker*, 968 P.2d 281, 286 (Mont. 1998); *Conklin by Johnson-Conklin v. MacMillan Oil Co.*, 557 N.W.2d 102, 105 (Iowa App. 1996); *Brown v. Brown*, 215 S.E.2d 671, 673 (Ga. 1975).

[20] *See, e.g., Smith v. Smith*, 966 A.2d 109, 114 (R.I. 2009); *Torres v. Com. Dept. of Public Welfare*, 393 A.2d 1079, 1080 (Pa. Cmwlth. 1978).

[21] *See, e.g., Wilkins v. Wilkins*, 48 P.3d 644, 649 (Idaho 2002); *Aaberg By and Through Aaberg v. Aaberg*, 512 So.2d 1375, 1376 (Ala. 1987); *People v. Lucero*, 747 P.2d 660, 663 (Colo. 1987); Utah Code Ann. § 30-1-4.5 (1987).

[22] *In re Estate of Bourassa*, 949 A.2d 704, 706 (N.H. 2008) (holding that New Hampshire law requires a minimum 3-year period of cohabitation). *See also* N.H. Rev. Stat. § 457:39 (2009).

[23] *See, e.g., In re Estate of Smith*, 2009 WL 1532555, *1 (Ga. App. 2009); *Mueggenborg v. Walling,* 836 P.2d 112, 113 (Okla. 1992); *Nestor v. Nestor*, 472 N.E.2d 1091, 1094-1095 (Ohio 1984). *See also* Tex. Fam. Code. Ann. § 2.401 (2009) (providing that if the parties have been separated and ceased living together for a period of two years, "it is rebuttably presumed that the parties did not enter into an agreement to be married.").

[24] *See, e.g., Driscoll v. Driscoll*, 552 P.2d 629, 632 (Kan. 1976) (holding that "sporadic cohabitation" is not sufficient to establish a common-law marriage.).

[25] *Davis v. State*, 103 P.3d 70, 82 (Okla. Cr. App. 2004) (requiring "a permanent relationship, an exclusive relationship."); *Beck v. Beck*, 246 So.2d 420, 425 (Ala. 1971) ("to constitute such a marriage there must first have been a present agreement, a mutual understanding to presently enter into the marriage relationship, permanent and exclusive of all others.").

[26] *See, e.g., Winfield v. Renfro*, 821 S.W.2d 640, 646-648 (Tex. App. 1991).

[27] *See, e.g., In re Estate of Burroughs*, 486 N.W.2d 113, 116 (Mich. App. 1992) (applying Texas law) (holding that "[l]iving together in Michigan does not satisfy the Texas cohabitation element.").

[28] *See, e.g.,* Utah Code Ann. 30-1-4.5 (1987); *Kowalik v. Kowalik*, 691 N.E.2d 1152, 1154 (Ohio 1997); *Chandler v. Central Oil Corp. Inc.*, 853 P.2d 649, 650 (Kan. 1993); *Brinckle v. Brinckle*, 12 Phila. 232, 234 (Pa. 1877).

[29] Tex. Fam. Code. Ann. § 2.401(a)(2) (2009).

[30] *Matter of Estate of Stodola*, 519 N.W.2d 97, 98 (Iowa. App. 1994).

[31] *See Gray v. Bush*, 835 So.2d 192, 194-195 (Ala. Civ. App. 2001); *Quinonez-Saa v. State*, 860 S.W.2d 707, 710 (Tex. App. 1993); *Whitworth v. Whitworth*, 54 So.2d 575, 577 (Ala. 1951); *In re Trope's Estate*, 124 P.2d 733, 735, 737 (Okla. 1942).

[32] *See, e.g., Butler v. Coonrod*, 671 So.2d 750, 752 (Ala. Civ. App. 1995); *Bolash v. Heid*, 733 S.W.2d 698, 699 (Tex. Civ. App. 1987); *In re Marriage of Grother,*

242 N.W.2d 1, 2 (Iowa 1976); *State v. Johnson*, 532 P.2d 1325, 1329 (Kan. 1975).

[33] *See, e.g., Welch v. State*, 908 S.W.2d 258, 265 (Tex. App. 1995); *In re Marriage of Gebhardt*, 426 N.W.2d 651, 653 (Iowa App. 1988); *Coleman v. Aubert*, 531 So.2d 881, 882-883 (Ala. 1988).

[34] *See, e.g., Winfield v. Renfro*, 821 S.W.2d 640, 648 (Tex. App. 1991).

[35] *See, e.g., In re Estate of Ober*, 62 P.3d 1114, 1117 (Mont. 2003); *Winfield v. Renfro*, 821 S.W.2d 640, 651 (Tex. App. 1991); *In re Marriage of Winegard*, 257 N.W.2d 609, 617 (Iowa 1977).

[36] *See In re Marriage of Winegard*, 257 N.W.2d 609, 617 (Iowa 1977). *See also* Montana Code Ann. 26-1-602(30) (2007) (a rebuttable presumption exists that a man and woman "deporting themselves as husband and wife have entered into a lawful contract of marriage.").

[37] *See, e.g., State v. Phelps*, 652 N.E.2d 1032, 1035 (Ohio App. 1995); *Winfield v. Renfro*, 821 S.W.2d 640, 651 (Tex. App. 1991); *Brown v. Brown*, 215 S.E.2d 671, 672 (Ga. 1975).

[38] *See, e.g., Sulfridge v. Kindle*, 2005 WL 1806482 (Ohio. App. 2005); *Matter of Estate of Vandenhook*, 855 P.2d 518, 520 (Mont. 1993); *Nestor v. Nestor*, 472 N.E.2d 1091, 1095 (Ohio 1984); *In re Marriage of Winegard*, 257 N.W.2d 609, 617 (Iowa 1977).

[39] *Beck v. Beck*, 246 So.2d 420, 426 (Ala. 1971). *See also* John B. Crawley, *Is the Honeymoon Over for Common Law Marriage: A Consideration of the Continued Viability of the Common Law Marriage Doctrine*, 29 CUMB. L. REV. 399, 405 (1998/1999); *Piel v. Brown*, 361 So.2d 90, 94-95 (Ala. 1978).

[40] *See, e.g., Brown v. Brown*, 215 S.E.2d 671, 672 (Ga. 1975).

[41] *See, e.g., In re Gholson's Estate*, 361 P.2d 791, 792 (Idaho 1961); *McArthur v. Hall*, 169 S.W.2d 724, 728 (Tex. Civ. App. 1943); *In re Trope's Estate*, 124 P.2d 733, 736-737 (Okla. 1942).

[42] *See, e.g., Callen v. Callen*, 620 S.E.2d 59, 62 (S.C. 2005); *Staudenmayer v. Staudenmayer*, 714 A.2d 1016, 1020-1021 (Pa. 1998); *In re Bragg's Estate*, 334 So.2d 271, 272 (Fla. App. 1976) (common-law marriage was recognized in Florida prior to January 2, 1968).

[43] *See* 20 C.F.R. § 30.111(b) (2007).

[44] *See* 73 Fed. Reg. 18553 (April 4, 2008).

[45] *Montana v. United States*, 450 U.S. 544, 564 (1980). *See also U.S. v. Jarvison*, 409 F.3d 1221, 1225 (10th Cir. 2005).

[46] *See* 9 N.N.C. § 8 (2009).

[47] Pueblo of Acoma Laws § 4-2-2 (2003).

[48] *Id.*

[49] *See* Federal (EEOICPA) Procedure Manual, Chapter 2-1200.5 (August 2009).

[50] *See* 20 C.F.R. § 30.111(a) (2007).

[51] *See* 20 C.F.R. § 30.111(c) (2007).

[52] *See* 20 C.F.R. § 30.111(a) (2007).

[53] *Commonwealth v. McLean*, 564 A.2d 216, 221 (Pa.Super. 1989) ("there is a rebuttable presumption of marriage where two essential elements exist: constant, not irregular or inconstant, cohabitation plus a broad and general, not partial or divided, reputation of marriage.")

[54] *See, e.g.*, Mont. Code Ann. § 26-1-602(30) (2007); *Wilkins v. Wilkins*, 48 P.3d 644, 649 (Idaho 2002); *Barker v. Baker*, 499 S.E.2d 503, 506 (S.C. App. 1998); *Crosson v. Crosson*, 668 So.2d 868, 872 (Ala. Civ. App. 1995); *Edwards v. Edwards*, 222 S.E.2d 169, 171 (Georgia 1975); *Tower v. Towie*, 368 P.2d 488, 490-491 (Okla. 1962); *Callen v. Callen*, 620 S.E.2d 59, 62 (S.C. 2005); *Jeanes v. Jeanes*, 177 S.E.2d 537, 539 (S.C. 1970).

[55] *See, e.g.*, *In re Marriage of Winegard*, 257 N.W.2d 609, 617 (Iowa 1977); *Young v. General Baking Co.*, 12 N.E.2d 1016, 1018 (Ind. 1938).

[56] Black's Law Dictionary, Ninth Edition (2009).

Appendix

I.   Common-Law Marriage States: Jurisdictions which recognize common-law marriages currently being established within their borders.

Alabama	Rhode Island
Colorado	South Carolina
Iowa	Texas
Kansas	Utah
Montana	District of Columbia
New Hampshire	Navajo Nation
Oklahoma	Pueblo of Acoma

II.   Recent Abolition States: Jurisdictions which recognize common-law marriages that were created within their borders prior to the date shown below, but do not recognize those created on or after that date.

Georgia (January 2, 1997)	Ohio (October 10, 1991)
Idaho (January 1, 1996)	Pennsylvania (January 2, 2005)

III.   Certified Marriage States: These jurisdictions do not recognize common-law marriages created within their borders and either abolished common-law marriage long ago or never recognized it. The dates denote the date of abolition for those states which abolished common-law marriage since 1920. Those states with no associated date either abolished common-law marriage prior to 1920 or never recognized it at all.

Alaska	Missouri (April 1, 1921)
Arizona	Nebraska (August 2, 1923)
Arkansas	New Jersey (December 2, 1939)
California	New York (April 29, 1933)
Connecticut	North Carolina
Delaware	North Dakota
Florida (January 2, 1968)	Nevada (March 30, 1943)
Hawaii (April 6, 1920)	New Mexico
Illinois	Oregon
Indiana (January 2, 1958)	South Dakota (July 1, 1959)
Kentucky	Tennessee
Louisiana	Vermont
Maine	Virginia
Maryland	Washington
Massachusetts	West Virginia
Michigan (January 2, 1957)	Wisconsin
Minnesota (April 27, 1941)	Wyoming
Mississippi (April 6, 1956)	

IV.   Source Law of Common-Law States and Recent Abolition States

Alabama

"Common-law marriages are valid in Alabama and are co-equal with ceremonial marriages." *Mattison v. Kirk*, 497 So.2d 120, 122 (Ala. 1986) (internal citations omitted). *See also S.J.S. v. B.R.*, 949 So.2d 941, 946 (Ala. Civ. App. 2006). "The elements of a valid common-law marriage in Alabama are well settled. They are: (1) capacity; (2) present agreement or consent to be husband and wife; (3) public recognition of the existence of the marriage; and (4) cohabitation or mutual assumption openly of marital duties and obligations." *Aaberg By and Through Aaberg v. Aaberg*, 512 So.2d 1375, 1376 (Ala. 1987). "[I]n order to constitute a valid common-law marriage, the man and woman, following their mutual consent to live as man and wife, must so live as to gain the recognition of the public that they are living as man and wife rather than in a state of concubinage." *Beck v. Beck*, 246 So.2d 420, 426 (Ala. 1971). "[T]o constitute such a marriage there must first have been a present agreement, a mutual understanding to presently enter into the marriage relationship, permanent and exclusive of all others." *Beck*, 246 So.2d at 425. Finally, "[a] marriage contract is of no validity if either of the contracting parties is of unsound mind." *Id.*

Colorado

Colorado recognizes common-law marriages contracted within the state. Colo. Rev. Stat. Ann. § 14-2-104 (2009). *In re Marriage of J.M.H. & Rouse,* 143 P.3d 1116, 1117 (Colo. App. 2006); *In re the Marriage of Phelps and Robinson*, 74 P.3d 506, 509-510 (Colo. App. 2003). *See also* Colo. Rev. Stat. Ann. §§ 14-2-112, 14-2-109.5, 14-2-110. In general, a common-law marriage in Colorado is established by the mutual consent of the parties, *e.g.*, mutual consent or agreement of the parties to be husband and wife, followed by their mutual and open assumption of a marital relationship. *People v. Lucero*, 747 P.2d 660, 663 (Colo. 1987). "The two factors that most clearly show an intention to be married are cohabitation and a general understanding or reputation among persons in the community in which the couple lives that the parties hold themselves out as husband and wife." *Lucero*, 747 P.2d at 665. All common-law marriages entered into in Colorado on or after September 1, 2006 are only valid if each party is eighteen years of age or older. *See* Colo. Rev. Stat. Ann. §§ 14-2-104, 14-2-109.5.

Georgia

"Although Georgia does not recognize common-law marriages entered into after January 1, 1997, otherwise valid common-law marriages entered into prior to January 1, 1997. . .shall continue to be recognized in this state." *In re Estate of Smith*, 2009 WL 1532555, *1 (Ga. App. 2009) (internal quotations omitted). *See also* Ga. Code Ann. § 19-3-1.1 (2009). For a party to prove the existence of common-law marriage in Georgia, that party must prove the following elements: (1) the parties must be able to contract; (2) the parties must agree to live together as man and wife; and (3) the parties must consummate the agreement. *See Estate of Smith, supra*, 2009 WL 1532555 at *1; *Brown v. Brown*, 215 S.E.2d 671, 672 (Ga. 1975). Further, "[a] legal marital relationship cannot be partial or periodic." *Estate of Smith*, 2009 WL 1532555 at *1. The Supreme Court of Georgia has held that proving the existence of an "actual contract. . . may be done by [submitting evidence that shows] such circumstances as the act of living together as man and wife, holding themselves out to the world as such, and repute in the vicinity and among neighbors and visitors that they are such, and, indeed, all such facts as usually accompany the marriage relation and indicate the factum of marriage." *Brown, supra*, 215 S.E.2d at 673.

Idaho

Idaho recognizes common-law marriages that were established in Idaho prior to January 1, 1996, but does not recognize common-law marriages claimed to be established in Idaho on or after that date. Idaho Code §§ 32-201, 32-301 (2009); *Wilkins v. Wilkins*, 48 P.3d 644, 649 (Idaho 2002). "In order to demonstrate the existence of a common-law marriage, the evidence must show that the parties were both capable of giving consent, and did in fact consent, to the common law marriage at its inception." *Wilkins*, 48 P.3d at 649. "The parties must assume the rights, duties and obligations of marriage." *Id.* "The parties' consent may be either expressed or implied by their conduct." *Id.* "If consent is implied, the best and most common, although not exclusive, method of proving consent is to show cohabitation, general reputation in the community as husband and wife, and holding oneself out as married." *Id.* "From such evidence, the court may infer that, at the outset, mutual consent was present." *Id.* "Because questions as to the existence of such a marriage frequently arise after the death of one party, common-law marriage may be proven by the testimony of only one surviving party." *Id.* "Once the parties to the alleged common-law marriage establish a prima facie case by a preponderance of the evidence, a presumption of marriage exists, which must be overcome by the opposing party with clear and convincing evidence." *Id.* "Once parties agree or consent to marry and consummate the marriage by mutual assumption of marital rights, duties and obligations, their subsequent actions cannot defeat the marriage, because there is no common-law divorce." *Id.*

Iowa

"Common-law marriage is recognized in Iowa." *In re Marriage of O'Connor-Sherrets and Sherrets*, 2008 WL 4877763, *1 (Iowa App. 2008); *Conklin by Johnson-Conklin v. MacMillan Oil Co.*, 557 N.W.2d 102, 105 (Iowa App. 1996). When one party is deceased, the party asserting the marriage must prove the elements of a common-law marriage by a preponderance of clear, consistent, and convincing evidence. *Conklin*, 557 N.W.2d at 105. "In order to establish a common-law marriage, three elements must be proven: (1) present intent and agreement to be married, (2) continuous cohabitation, and (3) public declaration that the parties are husband and wife." *Sherrets*, *supra*, 2008 WL at *1; *Conklin*, 557 N.W.2d at 105. "Proof of cohabitation, as well as evidence of conduct and general repute in the community where the parties reside, tends to strengthen the showing of present agreement to be husband and wife, as well as bearing upon the question of intent." *Conklin*, 557 N.W.2d at 105. "Circumstantial evidence may be relied upon to demonstrate a common-law marriage." *Id.* A continuous cohabitation of the parties and the declaration or holding out to the public they were, in fact, husband and wife constitutes circumstantial evidence which tends to create a fair presumption that a common-law marital relationship existed. *In re Marriage of Winegard*, 257 N.W.2d 609, 617 (Iowa 1977). "An element essential to the proof of such relationship is a general and substantial 'holding-out' or open declaration to the public by both parties." *Id.* "In fact, such 'holding-out' or open declaration to the public has been said to be the acid test." *Id.* "In other words, there can be no secret common-law marriage." *Id.*

Kansas

Kansas has long recognized common-law marriage, but both parties must be at least 18 years of age at the time the marriage is established. Kan. Stat. Ann. § 23-101 (2009); *Flora v. State*, 197 P.3d 904 (Ks. App. 2008). "The basic elements essential in establishing the existence of such marriage relationship are: (1) capacity of the parties to marry, (2) a present marriage agreement, and (3) a holding out of each other as husband and wife to the public." *Sullivan v. Sullivan*, 413 P.2d 988, 992 (Kan. 1966). *See also Chandler v. Central Oil Corp., Inc.*, 853 P.2d 649, 652 (Kan. 1993).

Montana

The state of Montana recognizes common-law marriages. *See* Montana Code Ann. 40-1-403 (2007). In Montana, "the party asserting the existence of the common-law marriage must prove that: (1) the parties were competent to enter into a marriage; (2) the parties assumed a marital relationship by mutual consent and agreement; and (3) the parties confirmed their marriage by cohabitation and public repute." *In re Estate of Ober*, 62 P.3d 1114, 1115 (Mont. 2003). *See also Snetsinger v. Montana University System,* 104 P.3d 445, 451 (Mont. 2004). The Montana Supreme Court has also held that "A common-law marriage cannot exist if the parties have kept their marital relationship a secret. That is, to establish a valid common-law marriage, the couple must hold themselves out to the community as husband and wife." *In re Estate of Ober*, 62 P.3d at 1117. A rebuttable presumption exists that "[a] man and woman deporting themselves as husband and wife have entered into a lawful contract of marriage." *See* Montana Code Ann. 26-1-602(30) (2007). Montana courts recognize a public policy that favors the finding of a valid marriage and they have no requirement that the wife assume her husband's last name in order to establish a common-law marriage. *In re Estate of Ober*, 62 P.3d at 1117.

New Hampshire

"New Hampshire is a jurisdiction which does not recognize the validity of common-law marriages except to the limited extent provided by RSA 457:39." *In re Estate of Bourassa*, 949 A.2d 704, 706 (N.H. 2008). "Pursuant to that statute, which has been in substantially the same form since 1842, persons cohabiting and acknowledging each other as husband and wife, and generally reputed to be such, for the period of 3 years, and until the decease of one of them, shall thereafter be deemed to have been legally married." *Estate of Bourassa*, 949 A.2d at 706 (internal quotations omitted); N.H. Rev. Stat. § 457:39 (2009). *See also Delisle v. Smalley,* 96 N.H. 58, 59, 69 A.2d 868 (1949).

Ohio

Ohio law recognizes common-law marriages contracted in that state, but only if they came into existence prior to October 10, 1991. *Gearhart v. Gearhart*, 2008 WL 62286, *2 (Ohio App. 2008); *State v. Phelps*, 652 N.E.2d 1032, 1035 (Ohio App. 1995). *See also* Ohio Rev. Code Ann. § 3105.12 (2009). The elements of a common-law marriage in Ohio are: (1) an agreement *in praesenti* (at the present time rather than at a future time) to enter into a mutual contract to take each other as man and wife, when made by parties competent to contract; (2) accompanied and followed by cohabitation as husband and wife; and (3) a holding out by the parties to those with whom they normally come into contact, resulting in a reputation as a married couple in the community. *Phelps*, 652 N.E.2d at 1035; *Nestor v. Nestor*, 472 N.E.2d 1091, 1094 (Ohio 1984). "Secret cohabitation with its attendant indicium of concealment concerning the sexual activity of the parties will not suffice as evidence of a valid common law marriage." *Nestor*, 472 N.E.2d at 1095. "Because common-law marriages have always been disfavored in Ohio, the party asserting the marriage's existence had the burden to prove those elements by clear and convincing evidence." *Gearhart*, 2008 WL at *3 (citing *Nestor*, 472 N.E.2d at 1094). The Ohio Supreme Court in *Nestor* also clarified that:

> The agreement to marry *in praesenti* is the essential element of a common-law marriage. Its absence precludes the establishment of such a relationship even though the parties live together and openly engage in cohabitation . . . .
>
> The contract of marriage *in praesenti* may be proven either by way of direct evidence which establishes the agreement, or by way of proof of cohabitation, acts, declarations, and the conduct of the parties and their recognized status in the community in which they reside.

Nestor, 472 N.E.2d at 1094.

Oklahoma

Oklahoma recognizes common-law marriages established within its borders. *See Standefer v. Standefer,* 26 P.3d 104, 107 (Okla. 2001); *Davis v. State*, 70 (Okla. Crim. App. 2004). The elements necessary to establish a common-law marriage in Oklahoma are: (1) an actual and mutual agreement between the spouses to be husband and wife; (2) a permanent relationship as man and wife; (3) an exclusive relationship (which may be proved by cohabitation) as man and wife; and (4) the parties to the marriage must hold themselves out publicly as husband and wife. *Stinchcomb v. Stinchcomb*, 674 P.2d 26, 28-29 (Okla. 1983); *Estate of Phifer*, 629 P.2d 808, 809 (Okla. App. Ct. 1981). Thus, a common-law marriage is established if competent parties enter the relationship by mutual agreement, exclusive of all others, and consummate the arrangement by cohabitation and open assumption of marital duties. *Mueggenborg v. Walling,* 836 P.2d 112, 113 (Okla. 1992). Open and notorious cohabitation is evidence of a marriage agreement, other elements being present, while lack of such open cohabitation may be evidence tending to discredit the alleged agreement, thus casting upon the alleging party a greater burden in the actual proof of the agreement. *Mueggenborg*, 836 P.2d at 113 n.2. The person seeking to establish the existence of a common-law marriage in Oklahoma has the burden to show its existence by clear and convincing evidence. *Standefer*, 26 P.3d at 107. However, the relationship may be proved by both direct and circumstantial evidence. *Maxfield v. Maxfield*, 258 P.2d 915, 921 (1953).

Pennsylvania

The Pennsylvania legislature recently abolished common-law marriages contracted after January 1, 2005:

> No common-law marriage contracted after January 1, 2005, shall be valid. Nothing in this part shall be deemed or taken to render any common-law marriage otherwise lawful and contracted on or before January 1, 2005, invalid.

23 Pa. Cons. Stat. Ann. § 1103 (2008). Thus, such marriages established in Pennsylvania on or before January 1, 2005 are valid and recognized. Under Pennsylvania law, "[a] common-law marriage can only be created by an exchange of words in the present tense, spoken with the specific purpose that the legal relationship of husband and wife is created by that." *Staudenmayer v. Staudenmayer*, 714 A.2d 1016, 1020-1021 (Pa. 1998). Pennsylvania law requires "a positive mutual agreement, permanent and exclusive of all others, to enter into a marriage relationship, cohabitation sufficient to warrant a fulfillment of necessary relationship of man and wife, and an assumption of marital duties and obligations." *Staudenmayer*, 714 A.2d at 1020. "[C]ohabitation of the parties and the reputation that they are married do not, in themselves, constitute a marriage, they constitute evidence from which a marriage may be found." *Torres v. Com. Dept. of Public Welfare*, 393 A.2d 1079, 1080 (Pa. Cmwlth. 1978).

> We have allowed, as a remedial measure, a rebuttable presumption in favor of a common-law marriage based on sufficient proof of cohabitation and reputation of marriage where the parties are otherwise disabled from testifying regarding *verba in praesenti*. However, where the parties are available to testify regarding *verba in praesenti,* the burden rests with the party claiming a common-law marriage to produce clear and convincing evidence of the exchange of words in the present tense spoken with the purpose of establishing the relationship of husband and wife, in other words, the marriage contract. In those situations, the rebuttable presumption in favor of a common-law marriage upon sufficient proof of constant cohabitation and reputation for marriage, does not arise.

Staudenmayer, 714 A.2d at 1020-1021.

> We note the Pennsylvania courts' reluctance to validate a common-law marriage where words *in praesenti* are absent and proof of reputation and cohabitation is lacking, for

"[w]hen the lips of a man are sealed by death, and he leaves
no satisfactory evidence as to the existence of such contract,
courts will be very slow to establish it in derogation of the
undoubted rights of those who follow him."

In re Estate of Rees, 480 A.2d 327, 328 (Pa. Super. 1984).

Rhode Island

"This state recognizes common-law marriage." *Smith v. Smith*, 966 A.2d
109, 114 (R.I. 2009). "[T]o establish a common-law marriage, we have
adopted the clear and convincing standard of proof." *Smith*, 966 A.2d at
114. "A common-law marriage requires evidence that the parties
seriously intended to enter into the husband-wife relationship." *Id.*
(internal quotations omitted). "In addition, the conduct of the parties must
be of such a character as to lead to a belief in the community that they
were married." *Id.* "The elements of intent and belief are demonstrated
by inference from cohabitation, declarations, reputation among kindred
and friends, and other competent circumstantial evidence." *Id.* "Although
intent may be inferred from cohabitation, declarations, reputation, and
other competent evidence. . .cohabitation alone is not conclusive of intent
to be husband and wife, and such evidence may be rebutted by counter-
proof." *Id.* "Furthermore, it is required that the parties must *mutually* and
presently intend to be husband and wife rather than merely become
engaged to be husband and wife at some point in the future." *Id.*
(emphasis in original).

South Carolina

South Carolina currently recognizes common-law marriages. S.C. Code
1976 § 20-1-360 (2008); *Callen v. Callen*, 620 S.E.2d 59, 62 (S.C. 2005).
A common-law marriage in South Carolina must be proven by a
preponderance of the evidence. *Callen*, 620 S.E.2d at 62; *Kirby v. Kirby*,
241 S.E.2d 415, 416 (S.C. 1978). "A common-law marriage is formed
when two parties contract to be married." *Callen*, 620 S.E.2d at 62. "No
express contract is necessary; the agreement may be inferred from the
circumstances." *Id.* "The fact finder is to look for mutual assent: the
intent of each party to be married to the other and a mutual understanding
of each party's intent." *Id.* Courts have held that the facts and
circumstances must show an intention on the part of both parties to enter
into a marriage contract, and is usually evidenced by a public and
unequivocal declaration by the parties. *Owens v. Owens*, 466 S.E. 2d 373,
375 (S.C. Ct. App. 1996). "Further, when the proponent proves that the
parties participated in 'apparently matrimonial' cohabitation, and that
while cohabiting the parties had a reputation in the community as being
married, a rebuttable presumption arises that a common-law marriage was

created." *Callen*, 620 S.E.2d at 62. The intent to be married is usually evidenced by a public and equivocal declaration of the parties, but that is not necessary; the necessary intent may exist without ever being publicly and formally declared. *Tarnowski v. Liberman*, 560 S.E.2d 438, 440 (S.C. Ct. App. 2002). Therefore, the existence of a common-law marriage is often proved by circumstantial evidence. *Barker v. Baker*, 499 S.E.2d 503, 507 (S.C. Ct. App. 1998). Effective June 11, 1997, parties must be at least 16 years old to enter into a common-law marriage in South Carolina. S.C. Code 1976 § 20-1-200.

Texas

Texas recognizes common-law marriages contracted within that state and there are three elements of a Texas common-law marriage: (1) the parties agreed to be married; (2) after the agreement, they lived together in Texas as husband and wife; and (3) while they were living together in Texas they represented to others in Texas that they were married. *Lewis v. Anderson*, 173 S.W.3d 556, 559 (Tex. App. 2005); *Winfield v. Renfro*, 821 S.W.2d 640, 643-645, 648 (Tex. App. 1991). *See also* Tex. Fam. Code. Ann. § 2.401(a)(2) (2009). All three required elements must occur concurrently and must co-exist, *i.e.*, although they may initially arise at different times, they must all exist at the same time in order to establish a common-law marriage under Texas law. *Winfield*, 821 S.W.2d at 645-646, 648, 653. To establish the first element, "the evidence must show that the parties intended to have a present, immediate and permanent marital relationship and that they did in fact agree to be husband and wife." *Winfield*, 821 S.W.2d at 645; *Eris v. Phares*, 39 S.W.3d 708, 714 (Tex. App. 2001). However, the existence of this agreement may be inferred from evidence of the cohabitation and representations of the parties. *Winfield*, 821 S.W.2d at 646. And, an agreement to be married may be proved by direct or circumstantial evidence. *Russell v. Russell*, 865 S.W.2d 929, 933 (Tex. 1993). To establish the second element, the evidence must show that the parties lived together in Texas as husband and wife; cohabitation in another state is insufficient to establish the second element. *Winfield*, 821 S.W.2d at 646-648. To establish the third element, the parties must represent to others in Texas that they are married; representing to others in another state that they are married does not establish this element. *Winfield*, 821 S.W.2d at 648-651. Spoken words are not required to establish the third element; it can be established by conduct and actions of the parties. *Winfield*, 821 S.W.2d at 648; *Eris*, 39 S.W.3d at 715. But, the marriage must be "widely known in the community" and "occasional introductions as husband and wife do not establish the element of holding out." *Winfield*, 821 S.W.2d at 651. Proof of cohabitation and representations to others in Texas that they were married may constitute circumstantial evidence of an agreement to be married. *Eris*, 39 S.W.3d at 715. Finally, if the parties have been separated and ceased living together for a period of two years, "it is rebuttably presumed that the parties did not enter into an agreement to be married." Tex. Fam. Code. Ann. § 2.401.

Utah

Utah recognizes common-law marriages, but only under very limited circumstances. Utah first repealed the doctrine of common-law marriage in 1888, only to later readopt it with the enactment of Utah Code Ann. (1953) § 30-1-4.5 on February 16, 1987. *See* Richards, *Turning a blind eye to unmarried cohabitants: A look at how Utah laws affect traditional protections*, 2007 Utah L. Rev. 215, 219 (2007). Prior to the enactment of § 30-1-4.5, "Utah did not recognize an unsolomnized relationship as a marriage, even though the parties to the relationship may have acted in other respects as spouses." *Layton v. Layton*, 777 P.2d 504, 505 (Utah App. 1989). Under Utah law, a marriage that has not been "solemnized" is legal if a court or administrative order establishes that it arises out of a contract between a man and a woman: (1) both of whom are of legal age and capable of giving consent; (2) who are legally capable of entering into a solemnized marriage under the law; (3) who have cohabited; (4) who have mutually assumed marital rights, duties and obligations; and (5) who hold themselves out and have acquired a general reputation as husband and wife. *In re Marriage of Kunz*, 136 P.3d 1278, 1282 (Utah App. 2006); *State v. Green*, 99 P.3d 820, 823 (Utah 2004); Utah Code Ann. 1953 § 30-1-4.5(1). The determination by the court or administrative body must take place during the relationship or within one year following the termination of the relationship, including by death of one of the spouses. *Kunz*, 136 P.3d at 1282; *Green*, 99 P. 2d at 823; *Gonzalez v. Gonzalez*, 1 P.3d 1074, 1079 (Utah 2000); Utah Code Ann. 1953 § 30-1-4.5(2). Another Utah statute permits a court to enter an order *nunc pro tunc* establishing a valid marriage more than one year following the termination of the relationship, if the court finds that there is good cause to do so. *Behrman v. Behrman*, 139 P.3d 307, 310-311 (Utah App. 2006); Utah Code Ann. 1953 § 30-4a-1. However, if there is no order establishing that a common-law marriage exists, the State of Utah will not recognize the relationship as a legal and valid marriage. *See Kunz*, 136 P.3d at 1282; *Behrman*, 139 P. 3d at 310-311; *Green*, 99 P. 2d at 823.

District of Columbia

Common-law marriage has long been recognized in the District of Columbia. *Authentic Home Improvements v. Mayo*, 2006 WL 2687533, *4 (D.C. Super. 2006); *Coates v. Watts*, 622 A.2d 25, 27 (D.C. 1993); *Hoage v. Murch Bros. Construction Co.*, 50 F.2d 983 (1931). "The elements of common-law marriage in this jurisdiction are cohabitation as husband and wife, following an express mutual agreement, which must be in words of the present tense." *Coates*, 622 at 27 (citing *East v. East*, 536

A.2d 1103, 1105 (D.C.1988)). "Since ceremonial marriage is readily available and provides unequivocal proof that the parties are husband and wife, claims of common-law marriage should be closely scrutinized, especially where one of the purported spouses is deceased and the survivor is asserting such a claim to promote his financial interest. *Coates*, 622 at 27. "The burden is on the proponent to prove, by a preponderance of the evidence, all of the essential elements of a common-law marriage." *Id.*

Navajo Nation

The Navajo Nation recognizes common-law marriages established between members of the Navajo tribe. Section 3 of Title 9 of the Navajo Nation Code sets forth the elements of a common-law marriage as follows: "1. Present intention of the parties to be husband and wife; 2. Present consent between the parties to be husband and wife; 3.Actual cohabitation; and 4. Actual holding out of the parties within their community to be married." *See also United States v.* Jarvison, 409 F.3d 1221, 1225-1228 (10th Cir. 2005); *Beller v. United States*, 221 F.R.D. 679, 682 (D.N.M. 2003); *Navajo Nation v. Murphy*, 6 Nav. R. 10 (Nav. Sup. Ct. 1988).

Pueblo of Acoma Tribe

The Pueblo of Acoma tribe, like the Navajo Nation, is a federally recognized Indian tribe that recognizes the creation of common-law marriages among tribe members. Section 4-2-2 of the Pueblo of Acoma laws (2003) provides that "[a]ll marriages involving members of the Acoma Tribe shall be recognized if performed according to the laws of the state of their residence or according to tribal custom." Those laws also state that "[r]ecognition of a marriage by the Pueblo of Acoma will be shown on a certificate of marriage" and that a "marriage registry shall be maintained in the Acoma Tribal Offices." *Id.*